Understanding Great People of the Bible

An Introductory Atlas to Biblical Biography

Paul H. Wright

cartaJerusalem

Carta Jerusalem, Ltd.
18 Ha'uman Street, P.O.B. 2500,
Jerusalem 9102401, Israel
E-mail: carta@carta.co.il
www.carta-jerusalem.com

Cartography: Carta, Jerusalem

Photographs: Paul H. Wright

ISBN: 978-965-220-842-2

Printed in the United States of America

CONTENTS

List of Maps

Foreword

Great stories are told of great people, and in one sense all of the people of the Bible were great (some in their courage and faith; others in their rascality). The selection of people whose stories are traced here are typical of the whole, and touch on conditions common to all humanity. In this sense their stories transcend time and place. But they're also grounded in time and place, and it is this aspect that gives them a tangible sense of reality in which we, the readers, can see ourselves and the touch of God.

This work does not purport to be a history of ancient Israel, or even to provide material from which history, as it is commonly understood within the critical rigors of academia, should be written. Rather, it provides instead a summary of biblical data centered on the lives of some of the greatest characters who walked across the pages of scripture. More importantly, this retelling of various biblical stories weaves into the narrative flow a measure of the landed reality of the ancient Near East and eastern Mediterranean worlds that helps to fill in some of the interpretive gaps that plague all readers of the text. In doing so, it attempts to suggest reasons and consequences for human actions within the storyline, thereby "making sense" out of what might otherwise appear to be a too-brief or too-overly obtuse narrative. The goal is to help the reader see that whatever else the genre(s) or nature(s) of stories within the Bible might be, the characters within the stories are embedded within narrative parameters that define real time and space. By fleshing this material out in light of historic possibilities that actually attained in the ancient world, we can better appreciate the impact of these great people of the Bible in ours.[1]

(opposite) The Bible is full of stories of people striving to live secure and righteous lives in a land chosen by God. But not all of them defined what it meant to live righteously the same way. The biblical writers have given us a full repertoire of images drawn from nature describing both God and people. Among the most healthy is that of Psalm 52:8: "But as for me, I am like a green olive tree in the house of God; I trust in the lovingkindness of God forever and ever" (Ps 52:8). Though cut and pruned, the olive tree can survive for hundreds of years, ever renewed and green.

THE PATRIARCHS AND MATRIARCHS

As the ancestral head of a family that was to become "as numerous as the stars of the sky and the sand on the seashore" (Gen 22:17), Abraham is held in special regard by Jews, Christians and Muslims alike. It is therefore appropriate that his journeys tracked from one end of the Fertile Crescent to the other, across a great sweep of land that was to become so important in the rise and early history of today's three great monotheistic religions. At the same time, Abraham's journey from Mesopotamia (Gen 11:31–12:3) then to and from Egypt (Gen 12:10–13:1) anticipated later journeys that his descendants would make into and out of the same lands: the sojourn in Egypt, the Exodus and the Exile to Babylon (Gen 47:27; Ex 13:17–18; 2 Chron 36:20–23).

Although ancient Mesopotamia and Egypt were fertile lands, well watered by powerful rivers and offering social and economic opportunities the envy of the known world, Abraham was not at home in either. Instead, he was called to go to a thin, barren land between,[2] with few of the natural resources that are normally considered necessary for "the good life." His sojourns in the land of Canaan set the stage not only for the birth of two great peoples—the Jews through Isaac and the Arabs through Ishmael—but for the human journey taken by each one of his countless descendants through the uncertainties of life ever since (Heb 11:8–19).

Abraham's lifestyle bears certain important resemblances to Bedouin, at least Bedouin who inhabited the Middle East in pre-modern times. For millennia, large extended families of semi-nomadic pastoralists—herders of sheep, goats and cattle grouped along family and clan lines—have inhabited the thin band of arid land that lies between the Fertile Crescent and the inhospitable north Arabian Desert. Following the change of seasons in search of adequate pasturage for their animals, these families and clans would move and settle as needed. Most tended to stay within the limits of certain broadly defined territories and developed reciprocal relationships with persons in nearby towns or cities, exchanging goods and services and benefiting from mutually recognized water and grazing rights.[3] There is some evidence for occasional large-scale migrations from one region to another, however, and the movement of Terah with Abram (Abraham), Sarai (Sarah) and Lot from Ur of the Chaldees in Babylonia (southeastern Mesopotamia) to Haran at the upper arc of the Fertile Crescent (Gen 11:31–32), fits this pattern.[4]

Modern camel trekkers follow pathways through Transjordan similar to those known to Abraham, Isaac and Jacob. It was skills learned of the desert that bode the patriarchs well to receive—and keep—the promises of God.

Prompted by the divine call of God to go to a place known only as "the land that I will show you" (Gen 12:1), Abram left the relative security of Haran. Aging and childless, and lacking a son and now a home base, the two most essential resources for a semi-nomad, Abram journeyed into the unknown. Following the general line of the great trunk route connecting northern Mesopotamia to Egypt, he, his wife Sarai and his nephew Lot entered Canaan from the northeast. They camped on the outskirts of both Shechem and Bethel, two established city-states in the hilly center of the land, and offered due obeisance to the God who had promised *this* rocky landscape, of all places, to his descendants (Gen 12:4–8). We can assume that Abram's encampment at both places was rather lengthy and beneficial for all concerned, for no short-term visitor would be granted the right by the local inhabitants of the land to build an altar to a yet-unknown deity within their territory, the reality of his divine call notwithstanding.

From Bethel Abram and his not-yet-a-family journeyed south along the spiny central ridge of southern Canaan, a land fertile enough when the rainfall is good but that always lies at the doorstep of famine. His movement was slow and deliberate, paced by the speed of grazing sheep and goats, and he certainly interacted with people from every village and city-state along the way including Gibeon, Jerusalem, Bethlehem and Hebron, places critical to the later biblical story. This portion of Abram's journey ended in the Negeb, a largely barren expanse of fine, powdery soil that lacks sufficient rainfall for agriculture, tucked between the arable hills of Canaan and the dry Sinai desert (Gen 12:9). Although the biblical Negeb is suitable for a semi-nomadic lifestyle, a widespread famine soon forced Abram on to the fertile Nile delta in Lower Egypt. Here his initial attempts at establishing a symbiotic relationship with Pharaoh turned sour, and Abram had to be rescued by the hand of God, having nevertheless gained economically for the effort (Gen 12:10–13:1).

Upon returning to Canaan, Abram's growing band faced the consequences of denuding its grazing land and so split into two organic families, with Abram staying in the hills between Bethel and the Negeb and Lot descending into the Rift Valley near the Dead Sea. Lot eventually found grazing rights in the vicinity of Sodom (Gen 13:2–13), a fateful choice that would prove to be his undoing (Gen 19:1–29). The fiery destruction of Sodom and Gomorrah and return of the region to a salty wasteland eventually forced Lot's descendants farther east, into the lands that would one day become Moab and Ammon (Gen 19:30–38). Here the writer of Genesis, like later biblical authors, emphasized the geographical movement of persons from the land of promise back to the east, a route opposite that which Abram had originally come, as a way of setting apart both the divine choice of Abram's new land and the people meant to live in it (Gen 3:24; 36:1-43; 2 Kgs 24:14-15).[5]

For his part Abram remained in Canaan, moving alternately between the southern hill country around Hebron and the Negeb (Gen 14:13; 18:1; 20:1; 22:2; 23:2). He set up his main base of operations in the Negeb at a place called Beer-sheba (Gen 22:19), some distance east of the closest urban center at Gerar. At one point later in life, probably during another famine, Abram, who by then bore the covenanted name Abraham (which Genesis 17:1–8 takes to mean "father of a multitude") established his camp near Gerar (Gen 20:1). Although he had won grazing rights from Abimelech the king of Gerar, water remained a source of friction and prompted a formal alliance that recognized the rights of each within their respective territories (Gen 21:22–34).

ABRAHAM AND ISAAC IN THE LAND OF CANAAN

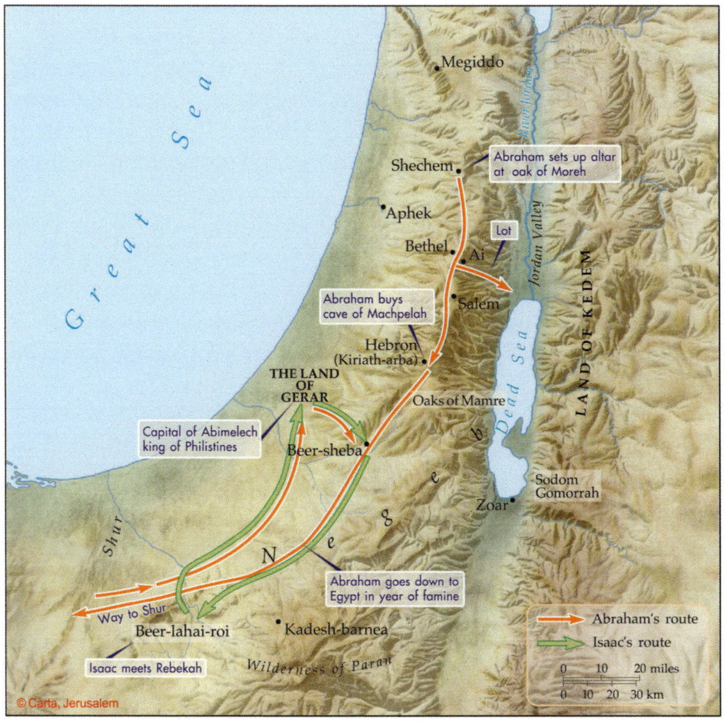

Abraham's longest journey after settling in Canaan was not for the benefit of his flocks, but as a man of war. The challenges inherent to daily survival in the harsh conditions of semi-nomadism foster survival skills that are best tested in war, and Abraham had his chance when an alliance of kings from Mesopotamia raided the territory of Sodom and Gomorrah, taking Lot and his possessions as war trophies (Gen 14:1–12). Abraham and 318 trained men of his household, a formidable fighting force, chased the Mesopotamian kings up the Rift Valley to Dan (Laish) and then on to Hobah, a location not yet identified with certainty but somewhere north of Damascus (Gen 14:13–16). Though in the vicinity of his extended family in Haran, Abraham returned to Canaan, pausing on his way to meet Melchizedek king of Salem (likely Jerusalem, a place that Abraham would have known from his prior journeys between Bethel and Hebron; Gen 14:17–24; cf. Ps 76:1). As a result of this meeting, Abraham's reputation and rights were strengthened in the central hill country.

But Abraham's arsenal of survival skills wasn't enough for he lacked what mattered most, a proper heir (Gen 15:1–2). The solution lay in the hands of God alone, and in two dramatic scenes which took place at unnamed locations somewhere in Canaan, Abraham received not only the divine assurance of a son born of him and Sarah (Gen 17:1–27), but of a real homeland for what would someday be an uncountable number of descendants (Gen 15:1–21). In the meantime, Abraham and Sarah had taken matters into their own hands, producing a son through Hagar, Sarah's maid (Gen 16:1–4). Though this was a culturally acceptable solution for a childless couple, it did create jealousies in the home and fell short of the divine promise (Gen 16:5–6; cf. Deut 21:15–17). Hagar and her son Ishmael fled toward Shur in the mid-Sinai, a wasteland barely fit for human habitation (Gen 16:7–15; cf. 20:1; 21:9–21). Exiled from the land of promise, Ishmael became the ancestor of the Arabs; the list of his descendants in Genesis 25:12–18 includes names of tribes and places known in the vast Sinai and Arabian deserts south and east of Canaan.

Finally, but in God's good time, a son was born to Abraham and Sarah (Gen 18:1–15; 21:1–7). Then came the bombshell—Abraham was to take Isaac to the land of Moriah and offer him as a burnt offering back to God (Gen 22:1–2). In a scene rich in the fabric of redemption, Isaac's life was spared (Gen 22:9–18) and with it the continuity of Abraham's family was again assured.

Sarah soon died and was buried in the Cave of Machpelah opposite Mamre (Hebron). Abraham purchased the cave from Ephron the Hittite, a local inhabitant of the land (Gen 23:1–20). Abraham refused an offer to use the cave free of charge; had he accepted Ephron's generosity, he would have been acknowledging that his descendants' rights to the land should remain under the authority of its indigenous inhabitants. Rather, by insisting that he purchase the burial cave outright, Abraham took the first legal step in providing an ancestral land for his descendants, in perpetuity. Abraham's grandson Jacob would continue the process by purchasing land in Shechem (Gen 33:18–20). Eventually Abraham, Isaac and Rebekah, and Jacob and Leah were all to be buried in this family tomb (Gen 25:9–10; 49:29–33).

Abraham's son Ishmael married an Egyptian woman (Gen 21:21), which was probably prudent given his mother's Egyptian bloodline (Gen 16:1) and that fact that he had been exiled from his father's house. But not so for Isaac, the child of promise! To maintain the strength of the family—as well as the integrity of the divine promise—it was essential that the heir marry within and keep the family's human and economic resources intact. For this reason, Isaac's wife had to come from among his closest relatives, the family of Abraham's brother back in Haran. Rebekah, Isaac's first cousin (once removed) willingly stepped into the role of matriarch-in-waiting (Gen 24:67) and followed Abraham's footsteps from Haran back to Canaan.

Upon the death of Abraham the responsibility of maintaining the family's welfare fell squarely on the shoulders of Isaac, no small task given the marginal climate of the Negev and the crucial need to protect the limited resources available there. Another famine drove Isaac west to Gerar, where the prevailing rainfall was predictable enough to support not only herding, but agriculture (Gen 26:1–6, 12–14). Isaac's skills at both, when blessed by the hand of God, tipped the local economy his way. Understandably threatened, Abimelech the king of Gerar rescinded the water rights that he had previously granted to Abraham, forcing Isaac to withdraw toward the desert but to a place still within the valley controlled by Gerar (Gen 26:15, 18; cf. 21:22–34). Taking matters into his own hands, Isaac opened a series of wells that his father had dug, reclaiming his family's rights to the land. In each case, the "Philistines" of Gerar successfully contested these rights, driving Isaac farther away. Finally, back at Beer-sheba, beyond Gerar's frontier and the limits of Abimelech's immediate economic interests, Isaac was able to camp without outside interference (Gen 26:18–25). With the balance of power restored in the Negeb, Abimelech reestablished with Isaac the covenant that he had previously made with Abraham (cf. Gen 21:22–34).

Meanwhile, Rebekah had given birth to twins. Destined to become two rival nations, Jacob (Israel) and Esau (Edom) already fought for territory in her womb (Gen 25:19–26). Esau, the firstborn, was very much at home in the brutish conditions of the Negeb, while Jacob, part by nature and part by his mother's coddling, preferred a homeland security akin to what Rebekah had left behind in Haran (Gen 25:27–28). Early on Jacob traded a common pot of lentil stew for Esau's birthright and so through the kind of trickery or cleverness that was (and still is) quietly admired in the art of Near Eastern diplomacy, moved into the slot of heir-to-the-patriarchy (Gen 25:28–34). Later, toward the end of Isaac's life, Jacob similarly grabbed the patriarchal blessing from Esau, and with it formal confirmation of his role as head of the family once Isaac had died (Gen 27:1–40).

JACOB AND HIS SONS

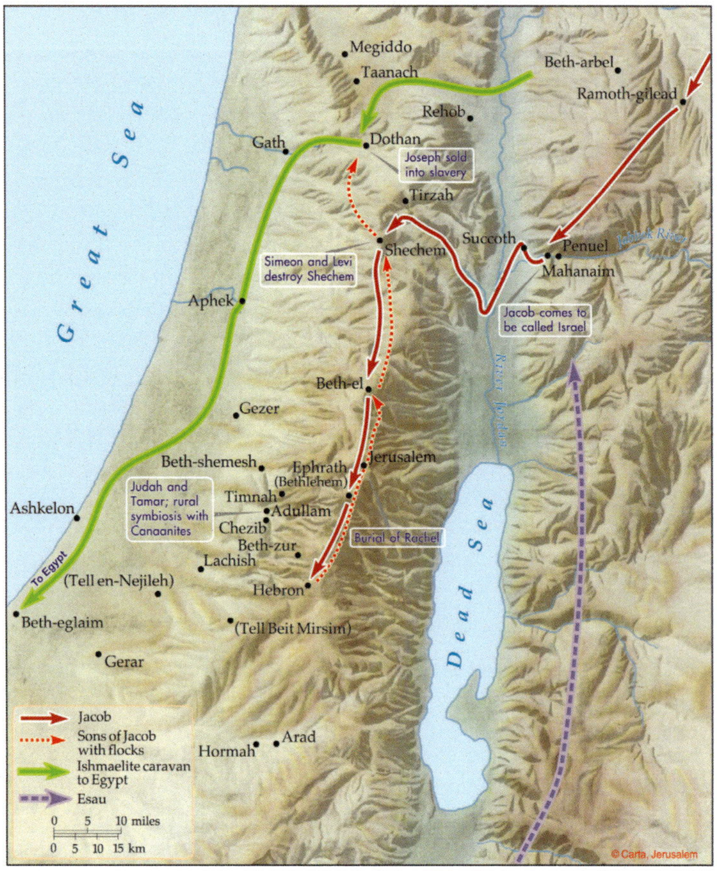

Predictably, Esau plotted to seize back his rights by force (Gen 27:41) and so Jacob fled, under the convenient suggestion of Rebekah, back to the land where a part of his mother's heart still lay (Gen 27:42–28:10). Arriving in "the land of the sons of the east" (Gen 29:1) near Haran, Jacob met Rachel, the daughter of Rebekah's brother Laban, at a well (Gen 29:2–12). This remains a classic "boy meets girl" scene typical of the ageless world of semi-nomadism. By means of the expectations that came with hospitality and negotiation, Jacob attached himself to Laban's household, first as a worker and then as a son, twice over. Typically a man in Isaac's position, already an heir, would take his new bride back to his own home, but the expediency of the moment—his own survival and a chance to marry well—kept him in the neighborhood of Haran. Laban, who, like Jacob, was skilled in the clever art of survival, gained an upper hand on his guest in order to ensure that both of his daughters would receive a proper future, and so Jacob married the older, homely Leah as well as the younger, more beautiful Rachel (Gen 29:13–30).

Jacob stayed in Haran under the patriarchal authority of Laban for twenty years. These were good years, secure and full of opportunity. Jacob honed his skills in animal husbandry so that the flocks under his care multiplied and were strong, but did so at the expense of Laban (Gen 30:25–43). His family eventually numbered 11 sons and one daughter, with another son on the way (Gen 29:31–30:24; 35:16–20). These boys were to become the ancestral heads of the twelve tribes of Israel, and Jacob's deathbed blessing for each carried geographical information that matched the particular part of the land of Canaan where each tribe would one day settle (Gen 49:1–27).

In the end Laban's extended family had two heads: he by right and Jacob by practice. This was an untenable situation and so the family and its resources were divided, with Jacob and those under his care moving back to the land of his birth (Gen 31:1–55). An encounter with both the forces of Esau and God in the region of Gilead's Jabbok River left Jacob with a new name, Israel, explained as "one who strives *with* God" (Gen 32:22–32; cf. Hos 12:3–4).

By now both Jacob and Esau had become patriarchs in their own right and agreed to respect each other's rights and territory (Gen 33:1–17). Esau stayed east of the Rift Valley; his descendants spread throughout southern Transjordan and the northern Arabian Peninsula and can be traced among known tribal and city names in later centuries (Gen 36:1–43). Jacob's family headed west, stopping first at Succoth where the Jabbok River meets the Jordan, a lovely spot in the mid-Jordan Valley (Gen 33:17). From there he followed good grazing land up the Wadi Farah to Shechem, a well-established Canaanite city-state on a hub of hill country routes blessed with abundant water and fertile fields. Here Jacob settled for some time and gained a degree of permanent status by purchasing land and building an altar to *El-Elohe-Israel* ("God, the God of Israel"; Gen 33:18–19). Eventually, like Abraham before him (cf. Gen 12:6–9), Jacob moved on to Bethel, built another altar and continued south, settling in the vicinity of Hebron (Gen 35:1–27).

Jacob's family matured in the fresh climate of the Hebron hill country. The aging patriarch favored Joseph, the oldest son of Rachel, his favorite wife, as heir-apparent, a situation that was a continual thorn in the sides of the ten older brothers (Gen 37:3–11). As the years passed and his holdings grew, Jacob routinely split his flocks among his various sons, sending some one way and others another, according to the change of seasons and established grazing patterns. At one point Jacob's older sons drove their flocks to the fertile land around Shechem, then as far north as the picturesque valley of Dothan (Gen 37:12–17). Joseph, sent by Jacob to enquire of his brothers' welfare, caught up with his older siblings in Dothan. There Joseph was seized and sold to a passing caravan of easterners—Midianites and Ishmaelites who were tracking the trade routes of the ancient Near East, bound for the lucrative markets of Egypt (Gen 37:18–35).

Joseph ended up attached to the house of Potiphar, a high official in the court of Pharaoh who lived in Goshen (Gen 37:36; 45:10). Goshen lay in the northeastern Nile Delta, a region that had been infiltrated by West Semites—among them shepherds and others looking for a better life—throughout the mid-second millennium B.C. The 15th Egyptian Dynasty (c. 1650–1550 B.C.), composed of foreigners from southwest Asia whom the native Egyptians labeled *hekaw-khasut*, "rulers of foreign lands" (i.e., Hyksos), based its operations here, at Avaris (*Tell ed-Dab'a*), and many scholars who trace an historic Joseph find this context to be a comfortable, though unable to be proven, fit for his migration and rise to power.[6]

Realizing the advantages of living under the protection of the Egyptian royal house, Jacob and his family moved to Goshen to avoid a famine back home (Gen 41:46–45: 28). Jacob and his family rode out the famine in Egypt, then stayed—life was good there, after all, compared to the marginal hills and deserts of Canaan (Gen 47:1–48:22). When Jacob finally died he was buried back home in the Cave of Machpelah outside Hebron. His final resting place was a down payment on the promise that his descendants would someday return to that land of the living (Gen 50:1–21).

And so the story of the patriarchs and matriarchs ended where it began, with a divine promise that a special family would live on a special land under the promise and protection of God. This is the essence of biblical *shalom*, life lived the way it's supposed to be. Although in the end Abraham, Sarah, Isaac, Rebekah, Jacob, Leah, Rachel and Joseph all failed to realize the fullness of their God-given potential (Heb 11:13–15), their lives anticipated the struggles and hopes of future generations that can be traced from the pages of the Bible until today.

MOSES

Moses, the great lawgiver, prophet, intermediary and founder of the nation of ancient Israel, was born in the region of Goshen in the northeastern Nile Delta at a time when the protective rights issued by the Pharaoh to Jacob's family had been rescinded (Ex 1:8–22). At the time the descendants of Jacob, by now known as the "sons of Israel," were building for Pharaoh the royal cities of Pithom (perhaps *Tell el-Mashkhuta*) and Rameses (known as Pi-Rameses, "the City of Rameses" in Egyptian documents, probably *Tell ed-Daba'a*, the same site as the earlier Hyksos capital Avaris). Egyptian royal activity was prominent in the northeastern Delta during the New Kingdom's 19th and 20th Dynasties (13th–mid-11th centuries B.C.), when no less than 11 Pharaohs bore the name Rameses.[7]

It should not be assumed that the Egyptians had reduced the sons of Israel to the status of slaves akin to the kind of slavery that was prominent in the Greco-Roman. There is very little evidence of chattel slavery anywhere in the ancient Near East. Rather, comparative sources from Deir el-Medina, a New Kingdom workman's village adjacent to the Valley of the Kings in Upper (southern) Egypt, suggests that the sons of Israel were government workers who lived in self-contained villages under the control of supervisors (taskmasters) responsible to the Pharaoh.[8] Depending on local conditions life could be good, or hard, and although the basic needs of the workers were supplied (the sons of Israel had their own houses and a large amount of livestock—Ex 9:4; 10:9; 12:22, 38), they were at the beck and call of others in a foreign land and certainly didn't feel free (Ex 1:8–14; 5:1–23). Indeed, Egypt was not their home.

Moses, who was raised in the royal court, never forgot his Israelite identity. When he had the chance to intervene on behalf of his fellows, even to the extent of killing an offending Egyptian, he did so (Ex 2:11–14). Having fallen out of favor with Pharaoh as a result, this highly educated, urban sophisticate became a wandering fugitive in self-imposed exile, far beyond Egypt's harsh eastern frontier. Moses fled to Midian, the beautiful yet howling wasteland (cf. Deut 32:10) surrounding the Red Sea's Gulf of Aqaba/Eilat. There he became attached to the family of Reuel, high priest of Midian, married Reuel's daughter Zipporah and settled into the Abrahamic lifestyle of a semi-nomad. He was as distant from his cultured upbringing as he could be, but somehow more in touch with the land and lifestyle of his ancestors than ever before (Ex 2:15–25). It was somewhere in this wilderness, at "Horeb the mountain of God," that Moses had his first encounter with the God of Abraham, Isaac and Jacob (Ex 3:1–4:17).

The face of Rameses II in stone repose welcomes visitors to the Luxor Temple in Upper Egypt. Don't be fooled by the benevolent pose—that Rameses felt it necessary to be remembered so for all eternity implies that his actual character was likely the opposite.

Armed with the promise and power of God to redeem his people and bring them home, Moses returned to Egypt, a pilgrim in the unholy land of his birth (Ex 4:18–31). Moses' appointment was with Pharaoh, eye to eye, and their tug-of-war tested the iron wills of both men. Through Moses' steady hand God poured nine plagues onto Pharaoh, devastating the Egyptian economy, people and land. Each plague also attacked an important god in the Egyptian pantheon and the natural resource that that god controlled (Ex 7:1–10:29).[9] Finally with the tenth plague, the death of the firstborn heir to the throne, Pharaoh's will was broken.

After celebrating their newly found freedom with the first Passover, Moses led his people out of Egypt (Ex 11:1–12:37). The most direct route to Canaan followed the north Sinai coast. Called "the Way of the Land of the Philistines" in Exodus 13:17 and the "Horus Road" in Egyptian documents, this was not only the trade route between Egypt and Canaan but an established military road over which the New Kingdom Pharaohs regularly marched in triumph into southwestern Asia. From the City of Rameses Moses first led the sons of Israel northeast, toward this military route, then veered to the south (Ex 12:37; 13:17–14:2). To Pharaoh this looked like aimless wandering (Ex 14:3); for Moses, it was a brilliant strategic move aimed at avoiding direct combat in the region of Pharaoh's strength in favor of setting a trap that only the God of Israel could spring (Ex 13:17–18; 14:1–12). Moses' path led directly to the Reed (not Red) Sea, which, by its Hebrew name (*yam suph*) must refer to one of the relatively shallow, reedy Bitter Lakes between the Gulf of Suez and the Mediterranean. A strong east wind, blown as it were by the breath of God (cf. Gen 1:9; 2:7), divided the water; Moses and the sons of Israel passed safely through before the waters swept back over Pharaoh's now-helpless army (Ex 14:13–15:21).

The bearded, turbaned men between the feet of a prancing war horse depicted in this inscribed relief at the great temple at Karnak in Upper Egypt represent shasu *(Bedouin) defeated by the Egyptian army of Pharaoh Mernepthah, son of Rameses II. It is possible that these* shasu *represent the people of Israel, which Mernepthah claimed to have defeated in Canaan. If so, this is the earliest artistic representation of Israel known to exist, offering a view of a transitional, pre-settlement group that must have been typical of the wilderness wandering days as well.*

THE TRAVELS OF THE SPIES

With the military threat erased and a renewed faith for the journey ahead, Moses drove Israel into the "great and terrible wilderness" (Deut 1:19) of the Sinai Peninsula.

One of the more perplexing puzzles facing biblical historical geographers is tracing the route of the Exodus through the Sinai. Although dozens of places are mentioned (Ex 12:37; 13:20; 14:2; 15:22–23, 27; 16:1; 17:1; 19:2; Num 10:12; 11:3, 34–35; 12:16; 13:26; 14:25; 20:1, 22; 33:5–49; Deut 1:19), the locations of virtually all of them are unknown. Most were no doubt local names for water sources or natural topographical features, names now lost in the mists of time. Some, like Mt. Sinai, are identified through early church tradition, though over two dozen suggestions for Mt. Sinai have subsequently been proposed. Still, there is no overly compelling reason to reject *Jebel Musa*, the traditional site high in the crystalline mountains of southern Sinai Peninsula. The location of the oasis of Kadesh-barnea, where Israel camped "many days" (Deut 1:46; cf. Num 13:26; 20:1), is also known (*Ein el-Qudeirat*, just inside the modern Egyptian Sinai border) and Elath and Ezion-geber (Deut 2:8) were certainly somewhere at the northern end of the Gulf of Aqaba/Eilat (one of them was likely *Tell el-Kheleifeh*). However, because the locations of most of the rest of the sites in Moses' Sinai itinerary are largely guesswork, it is not surprising that many routes of the Exodus have been proposed.[10]

Sunrise from the traditional site of Mount Sinai, over the granite mountains of the southern Sinai Peninsula. The view erupts with divine majesty.
The LORD came from Sinai;
indeed, he dawned on them from Seir,
he shown forth from Mount Paran (Deut 33:2).

A stand of palm trees and desert pines at a site in the northwestern Sinai called Ayin Musa, Moses' Spring, by locals beckons travelers still today. This is, perhaps, Elim, "where there were twelve springs of water and seventy date palms" (Ex 15:27), where Israel camped after crossing the Red Sea.

In any case, from Mt. Sinai Moses led his people northeastward to Kadesh-barnea, a large perennial oasis within striking distance of Canaan (Num 13:26; Deut 1:19). From there representatives of each of the twelve tribes of Israel, including Joshua (from Ephraim) and Caleb (representing Judah), journeyed the length of Canaan, spying out the land of the Patriarchs from the Negeb and Hebron to Lebo-hamath north of Damascus (Num 13:1–24). The spies' report of a blessed, fertile land with strong, walled cities met with mixed reviews, and resulted in an initial assault into Canaan from the south that was repulsed by the Amalekites and Canaanites at Hormah, a city in the vicinity of Beer-sheba (Num 13:25–14:45).

Now nearly forty years of wilderness wandering lay ahead—not because the distance to Canaan was long or Moses got lost (although one could argue that Israel's heart was), but because all Israel, with their livestock, reverted to a semi-nomadic lifestyle, charged by God to follow the change of seasons from *wadi* bottom to *wadi* bottom. Much of this wandering, though within reach of the Kadesh-barnea oasis (cf. Num 20:1, 14), was in the section of the mid-Sinai that today is called *et-Tih* (lit. "the one who is lost"), a vast, rocky, flat and featureless landscape with few springs and no soil. For a people born and bred among the fertile villages and farms of Egypt this was an unbearable change, beyond their capacity for survival. Deep in the wilderness and in a position where he had no choice but to rely only on the strength of God and the help of a few close friends (cf. Ex 17:11–13; 18:24–27), Moses met the challenge of a lifetime.

The journey of the sons of Israel to the land of promise finally

On their approach through Transjordan to Canaan, Moses led Israel on the desert route east of Edom and Moab. They camped for awhile in the upper tributaries of the Zered, a wadi with a perennial flow of water (Num 21:12). Even today, Bedouin pitch their tents in the cleft of the Zered where water remains more plentiful than it is on the highlands above.

led them into Transjordan. Here the itinerary is more certain, as many of the place names on the route have been identified (Num 21:10–20; 33:41–49; Deut 1:1; 2:1–5, 8, 13–14, 24; 3:1, 8–17, 27–29). Three people groups, each related to the sons of Israel, were already settling in the fertile highlands of Transjordan: Moab, Ammon and Edom (cf. Gen 19:37–38; 36:1–43). These emerging nation states were strung along the King's Highway, the most logical route of travel through the land. Moses approached from the south, via Elath, then skirted both Edom and Moab by the more easterly desert route (Num 21:4–5; Deut 2:8; Judg 11:17–18; cf. 2 Kgs 3:8). By doing so he avoided needless conflicts over grazing and water rights, while finding plenty of pasture and water for Israel's livestock at the upper reaches of the Zered (*Wadi el-Hasa*) and Arnon (*Wadi el-Mujib*) ravines (Num 21:12–13).

Opposite the northern end of the Dead Sea Moses turned westward, toward the Plains of Moab. His route had to take him through the Tableland of Moab (the Medeba Plateau), a buffer zone between Moab, Ammon and Canaan that at the moment was controlled by a local king, Sihon of Heshbon. From the point of view of Sihon, the approach of a vast horde of hungry semi-nomads from the eastern desert was a threat that could be repulsed only by war (Num 21:21–32; Deut 2:26–37; Judg 11:19–22; cf. Judg 6:3–5). Upon defeating Sihon, Moses and the sons of Israel gained a valuable foothold at the doorstep of Canaan, established control over a portion of the King's Highway and found land suitable for the tribes of Reuben and Gad (Num 32:1–5, 33–36; cf. Josh 13:15–23).

Moses continued north through the highlands of Gilead, skirting west of the Ammonites to Bashan, a northern buffer zone between Ammon, Aram-Damascus (Syria) and Canaan. By defeating Og king of Bashan at Edrei (Num 21:33–35; Deut 3:1-11), Moses assured Israel's influence in northern Transjordan, a reality that would prove valuable during the days of the Israelite Monarchy when David, Ahab and others tried to check the advance of Aram-Damascus into the same region (cf. 2 Sam 10:15–19; 1 Kgs 22:1–40; 2 Kgs 9:1–13). Moses allowed part of the tribe of Manassah (the Jair clan) to settle in Bashan, and the region took the name Havvoth-Jair ("the tent-villages of Jair"; Num 32:33; 40–42; cf. Josh 13:29–31). Recognizing the strategic value of the Jordan Valley and the fertile western slopes of the Gilead mountains, Moses placed the tribe of Gad there as well (Num 32:33–36; cf. Josh 13:24–28). With his lifetime of anticipation nearly over, Moses' final view into the land of promise was from Mount Nebo (Deut 34:1–4). The best of all possibilities for his people lay just ahead.

THE FINAL APPROACH TO CANAAN

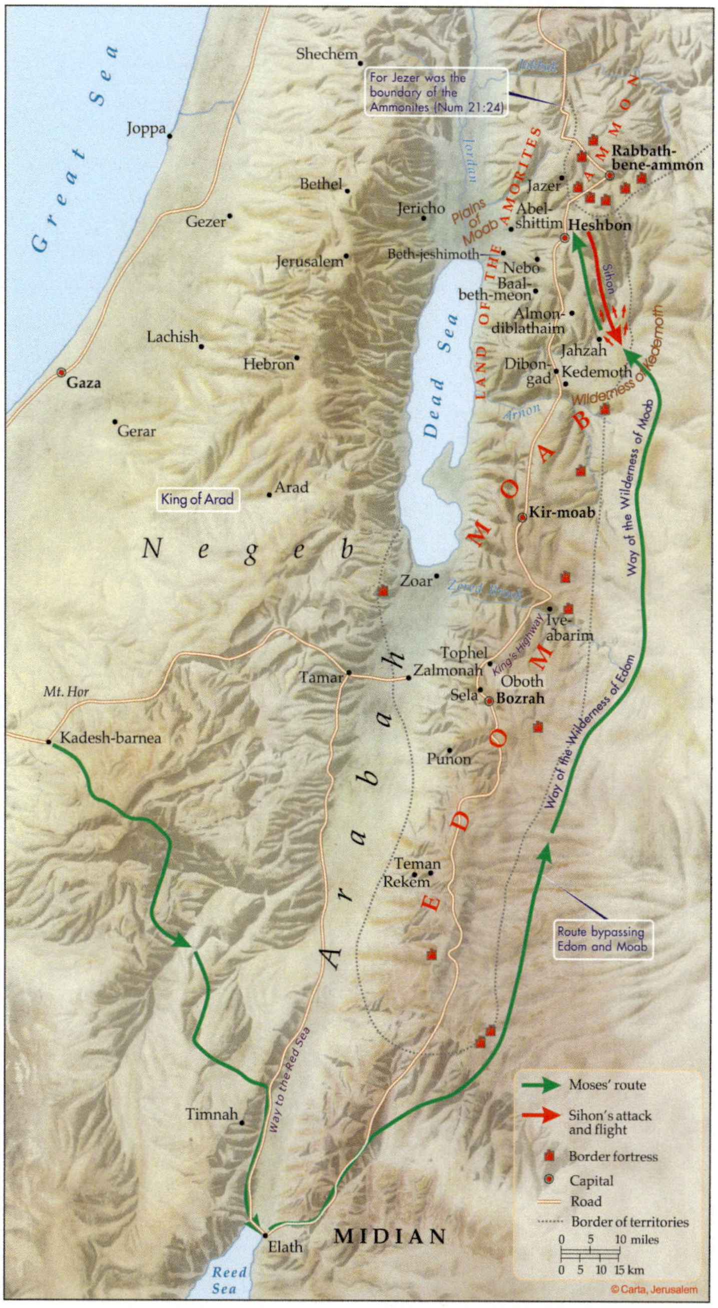

Moses' last view into the land of promise was from atop of Mt. Nebo. The traditional location of the mountain reveals the dramatic sweep of the Jordan Valley, with the rise of the hills of Judah and Ephraim beyond. The view beckons followers.

JOSHUA

Joshua had been the logical choice to succeed Moses since the early days of the wilderness wanderings—certainly since the death of Aaron—and it is possible to track the development of his leadership skills as he rose to prominence prior to Israel's entry into Canaan. Joshua had been with Moses everywhere, from the heights of Mt. Sinai (Ex 24:13; 32:15–18) to the daily toil of the tent (Ex 33:11). When Israel was just out of Egypt, moving vulnerably into the foreboding wilderness of Sinai, a young Joshua successfully repulsed a persistent attack by the Amalekites, desert raiders bent on easy spoil (Ex 17:9–16). He was part of a small contingent of men who entered Canaan from the south and traveled its full length, mapping the land in his mind as a reconnaissance for future conquest (Num 13:1–24). With Caleb, Joshua brought back a favorable report (Num 14:6–9), then withstood a popular uprising against his insistence that the land could be taken in spite of the great risks that conquest entailed (Num 14:10–38). As Moses led Israel on its final approach to Canaan nearly 40 years later, Joshua's role as second-in-command was formally ratified (Num 27:18–23). And although one might suppose that by now he was ready to assume the mantle of power, the biblical author underlined the need, at the very moment of Joshua's transition to the greater task at hand, for him to "be strong and courageous" (Deut 3:22, 28; 31:7–8, 14, 23; Josh 1:6–9).

Israel entered Canaan from the Plains of Moab, the southeastern, bulbous end of the Jordan River Valley lying just north of the Dead Sea. Opposite was Jericho, the City of Palm Trees (cf. Deut 34:3; Judg 1:16; 3:13), an oasis giving a bit of life to an otherwise stark and salty wasteland (cf. Jer 17:5–8). Beyond rose the sharp, rugged ascent of the Wilderness of Judah, a view that must have reminded Israel of the kind of landscape through which they had just traveled for most of a generation. But Joshua's vision was larger, and his experience in spying out the land thirty-eight years before confirmed God's promise that this indeed was "an exceedingly good land…a land flowing with milk and honey" (Num 14:7–8).

A victory at Jericho offered Joshua several strategic advantages as he sought to gain a foothold in Canaan. First, Jericho's destruction would ensure that Israel controlled the routes into the heartland of Canaan from the east, as well as those running between the fertile agricultural land of the northern Jordan Valley and the mineral wealth of the Dead Sea. Moreover, by taking Jericho, Joshua prevented an enemy at his back from hindering his further penetration into Canaan. Perhaps most importantly, although the city of Jericho was to be as thoroughly consumed as a burnt offering to God (Josh 6:21, 24), the oasis itself, fed by a powerful spring that still produces one thousand gallons of water per minute, remained fertile and would provide a wonderful base of operations as Israel pressed into the hill country.

JOSHUA'S THRUST INTO THE BELLY OF CANAAN

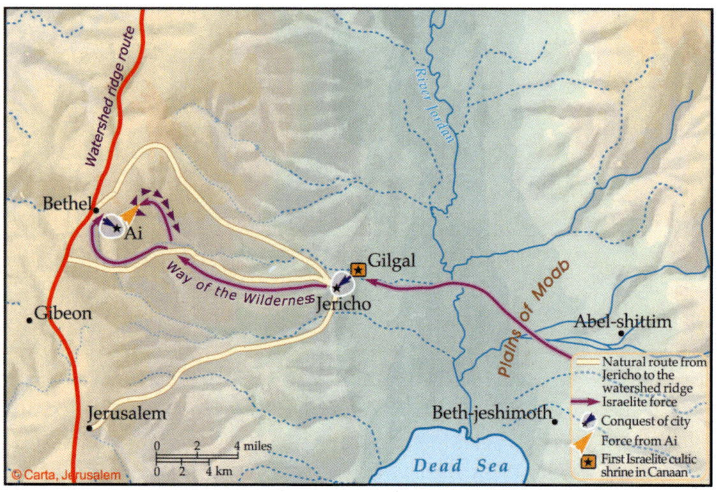

One of Joshua's primary goals upon bringing Israel into the land of Canaan was to recite the blessings of the covenant on Mount Gerizim (Deut 11:29; Josh 8:30–35). Here the green northern flank of Gerizim rises dramatically above the ancient site of Shechem (Tel Balata), today within the folds of the city of Nablus. Remains of a fortified temple tower in Canaanite Shechem dating to the Middle and Late Bronze Ages, the time of both Abraham and Joshua, dominates the foreground of the view.

The actual attack on Jericho cannot be explained in terms of rational military tactics, nor was it meant to be. Rather, this entire initial episode of conquest, from the time that Israel crossed the Jordan River at spring flood stage in full regalia with the Ark of the Covenant in processional lead (Josh 3:1–17) to the collapse of the city itself, must be seen as a mighty act of God. Nor should the lack of archaeological evidence corroborating the biblical description of the battle from *Tell es-Sultan*, the ruins of ancient Jericho, detract from the overall geographical common sense of the narrative account.

Joshua's next goal was to threaten the road running along the watershed ridge, the north-south lifeline connecting the all-important city-states of Hebron, Jerusalem, Gibeon, Bethel and Shechem. This he did by first taking Ai, a small satellite (cf. Josh 7:3) of Bethel which served as an advance outpost for the latter (Josh 8:1–29). He then moved directly up to Shechem, the main city-state of the central hill country, to renew the covenant of Sinai on Mounts Ebal and Gerizim (Josh 8:30–35; cf. Deut 27:2–8). Joshua's ability to penetrate into Shechem in the name of the God of Israel is admirable, yet puzzling, although it is likely that the men of Shechem, with long memories typical to the Middle East, acknowledged the right of the sons of Israel to reestablish roots in the area based on the old landed rights of Abraham and Jacob (Gen 12:6–7; 33:18–20). That the writer of the Book of Joshua did not include a battle account at Shechem might be explained on the principle that one shouldn't have to acknowledge a fight for what one believes is already theirs.

Having established a religious and nationalistic presence in the central hill country, Joshua in one sense had already met his goal—and too much so for the other city-states in the region. Most, naturally, sought to resist the Israelite advance (Josh 9:1–2); the

CUTTING THE FEET OUT FROM UNDER CANAAN

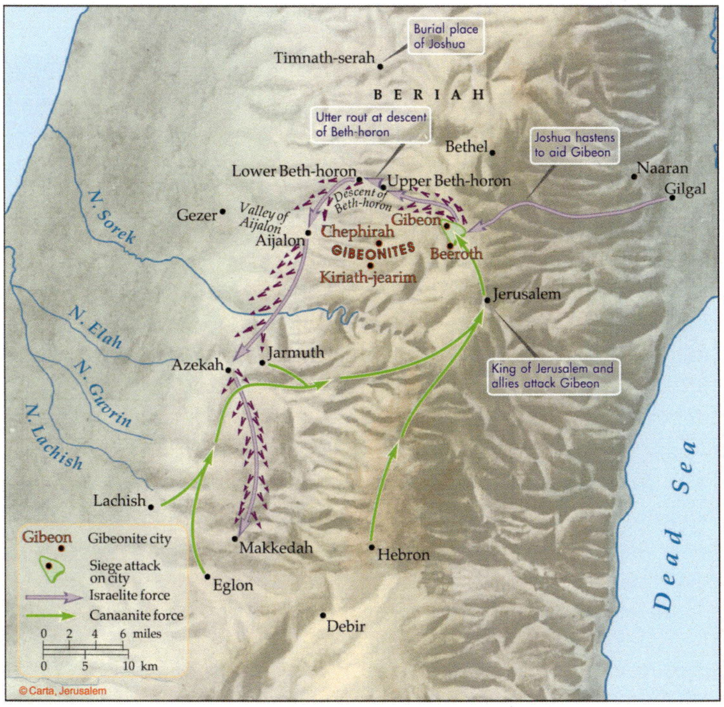

king of Gibeon had other ideas. The city of Gibeon dominated a wide spot on the watershed ridge midway between Jerusalem and Bethel, a plateau that was not only the upper terminus for routes coming out of Jericho but also one of the most important crossroads within the central hill country. Furthermore, Gibeon was the head of an alliance of cities that controlled the routes from the plateau westward toward the Shephelah (the western foothills) and coastal plain (Josh 9:17). Joshua made peace with the Gibeonites (Josh 9:3–15), then followed up by defeating an alliance of kings, headed by Jerusalem, that represented the entire southern region of Canaan (Josh 10:1–15). A mop-up campaign through the hill country and Shephelah established an Israelite presence throughout the region (Josh 10:16–43). From Jericho, Joshua had stuck a sword into the belly of Canaan, and with the defeat of the Jerusalem coalition, he undercut its feet. Only the head remained.

Joshua's final campaign was in the north, against the massive city of Hazor. In the Late Bronze Age, Hazor rivaled the great city-states of Mesopotamia in size and influence, as attested by both archaeological and textual (cuneiform) evidence.[11] Its location at the point where the great trunk route from the north enters Canaan, adjacent to the extraordinarily fertile Huleh Basin, ensured Hazor's dominance in the area. Anticipating the Israelite threat, Jabin king of Hazor pulled together a formidable coalition of city-states representing every sub-region in Galilee and controlling every important route and pass in the area; he was "the head of all these kingdoms" (Josh 11:1–4, 10). In a surprising move, this combined force rendezvoused not at one of the strategic valleys or passes in Galilee, but at the waters of Merom (Josh 11:5). The location of this meeting place is debated; some suggest the southern, swampy end of the Huleh Basin, others the spring-fed region of Mount Merom high in Upper Galilee. In either case, Jabin chose to leave Hazor open, apparently hoping that the Israelites would be drawn toward the city where they would be easily overrun by his chariot force. But Joshua, with courage from the hand of God, turned the tables and attacked suddenly, in an area—be it either swampy or rugged—where chariots were ineffective and the advantage quickly swung to the Israelite foot soldiers (Josh 11:6–9). Archaeologists have uncovered evidence that Hazor's large Canaanite palace collapsed in a particularly intense conflagration,[12] a circumstance in line with the biblical account of the nature of Joshua's attack (Josh 11:10).

Joshua's campaign through Canaan allowed him to claim the land for the people of Israel and the LORD their God, but many regions, especially the valleys and plains, were far from subdued (Josh 11:16, 23; cf. Josh 13:1; Judg 1:27–36). The focus of operations moved from Gilgal (Josh 14:6) to Shiloh, an isolated spot in the east central hill country where the Ark of the Covenant found a home and from which Joshua apportioned the entire land, subdued or not, among the Israelite tribes (Josh 18:1). Joshua, too, received an inheritance, at Timnath-serah in the fresh hills of the south-central hill country. His burial there, the burial of Eleazar the priest at Gibeah, and the internment of Joseph's bones on his purchased land in Shechem (Josh 24:29–33; cf. Gen 33:18–20) mark the end of the first phase of Israel's move into Canaan and the beginning of life in their promised homeland.

This lion, carved from a single huge block of basalt, is one of two that once guarded the entrance of a massive building in Canaanite Hazor. The style is clearly north Aramean, representing a cultural group that once dominated the northern part of the Levant as far south as ancient Hazor. For Joshua, Hazor represented the natural limits of Israel's northern expansion, and served to complete his conquest of the land of Canaan.

LOPPING OFF THE HEAD OF CANAAN

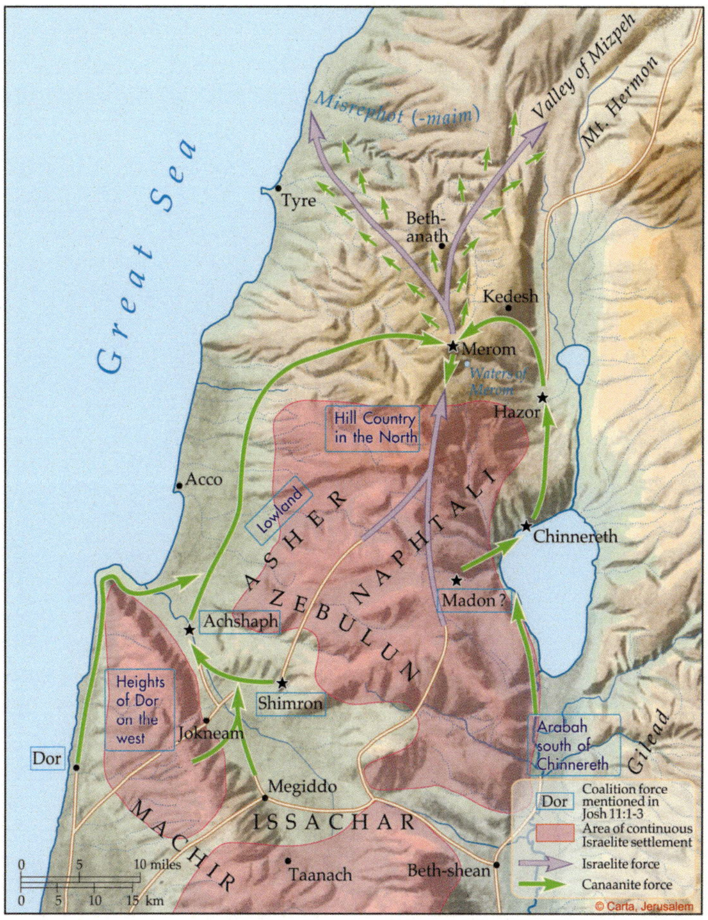

DAVID AND SOLOMON

The story of David and Solomon is inseparable from that of the rise of kingship in ancient Israel. Whoever aspired to rule all Israel in the 10th century B.C. faced two nearly insurmountable obstacles. Internally, the problem was a lack of unification among the tribes. The move from tribalism to monarchy carried enormous social, economic, political, religious and psychological ramifications, and was never completely made. Externally, the problem was weak borders, or, perhaps, a lack of realistic borders. The imperialistic Pharaohs of the Egyptian New Kingdom, who pretty much had had their way in Canaan throughout the Late Bronze Age (c. 1550–1200 B.C.), were in decline, and in their wake regional peoples such as Edom, Moab, Ammon, Aram-Damascus, Phoenicia and Philistia, in addition to Israel, found opportunity to express their own political and territorial ambitions. There was no simple answer to the question of how the Israelite identity, grounded to no small extent in a shared religious experience, would respond to and survive the challenges of tribalism and nationalism.[13]

Over time the Philistines posed the most persistent external threat to several of the Israelite tribes, and heroes such as Samson, Eli and Samuel were generally effective in checking their advance into the central hill country (Judg 13–16; 1 Sam 4; 7:3–12). It was natural that Israel's first king, Saul, was from the region of Benjamin, a Philistine "target" in the Israelite hills (1 Sam 9:1–10:27). All told, Saul's actions as a national leader were a good start, but largely ineffective to the overall task at hand (cf. the further Philistine incursion described in 1 Sam 13:1–14:23). At God's prompting, the aging Samuel chose David, of the tribe of Judah, as the next king (1 Sam 16:1–13). David represented a growing southern power base that included, among others, Simeonites (Josh 19:1–9; cf. 15:21–32), Kenites, Jerahmeelites, Calebites, Cherathites and Kenizzites (Josh 14:6; 1 Sam 27:10; 30:14).

David's first appearance in the public eye came as a direct result of the Philistine pressure on Judah in the Shephelah. By taking the upper, Judean end of the Elah Valley from Azekah to Socoh, the Philistines laid claim to the two main routes into the mid-section of the hill country from the west, one heading to Hebron, the primary city of Judah, and the other to Bethlehem and, eventually, Gibeah of Saul (1 Sam 17:1). Unchecked, they could walk into both, and Judah's viability as an Israelite tribe would be gone. Under-armed (cf. 1 Sam 13:19–22), undermanned (1 Sam 17:10–11, 16) and lacking the vision of the moment, Saul was paralyzed while David, with survival skills honed in the wilds of the Wilderness of Judah, defeated the Philistine hero in hand-to-hand combat (1 Sam 17:20–51). David's victory over Goliath allowed Israel to push the Philistines out of the Shephelah (1 Sam 17:52–53); his greater triumph was to gain a reputation as a warrior and leader mightier than even king Saul (1 Sam 18:6–9).

The view here is from one of the gates of Khirbet Qeiyafa toward Socoh, the lower, light green mound just right of center with the Elah Valley between. Another gate at Khirbet Qeiyafa points directly toward Azekah. Goliath and the Philistines camped somewhere between (1 Sam 17:1). A recent suggestion puts Saul's camp at Qeiyafa (1 Sam 17:20); if so, the famed confrontation between David and Goliath may have been at a point where the valley narrows a bit (the gai) at the base of Socoh.

Saul sensed that David's star was rising, and the two began a game of dodge and feint played out on a personal level but with tremendous national ramifications. While for Saul David could be useful (1 Sam 18:17–19; cf. 14:52), he was also a threat that needed to be neutralized. For David, Saul was God's anointed one (lit. "messiah"; 1 Sam 24:6; 26:9; 2 Sam 1:14) and should not be harmed, but at the same time David was not above forging alliances that strengthened his hand at Saul's expense. David became the captain of Saul's bodyguard (1 Sam 22:14) and also married Michal, Saul's daughter, for love but also out of expediency (1 Sam 18:20–30). The situation was endemic to tension and jealousy, prompting a prolonged flight and chase through the hill country, foothills and wilderness of Judah, taking him more than once even into Philistia (1 Sam 19:1–27:12).

It is clear that David's early experiences, both as a young shepherd and as a leader of men, strengthened his abilities, character and resolve to meet the more difficult challenges that he would face later in life. Many of the Psalms attributed to David speak of rough terrain, mighty rocks, strongholds and deliverers. David drew on a number of very tangible personal experiences to express his dependence on the power and provision of God in times of intense need (e.g., Psalms 18; 23; 31; 32; 37; 55; 61; 62; 63).

Israel's King Saul and Crown Prince Jonathan both lost their lives in an action designed to push the Philistines, who were bent on assuming the role of Egypt's heirs in Canaan, out of the Jezreel Valley (1 Sam 28:1–31:13). Worse yet, the Philistine action had cut the fledgling Israelite nation in two. With Israel on the brink of chaos, David pressed to seize control. First he was anointed king over Judah at Hebron by popular acclaim—one might say in triumph—and reigned from there for seven and one-half years (2 Sam 2:1–4, 11). Meanwhile, in Gilead Saul's general Abner orchestrated the

FACEOFF IN THE ELAH VALLEY: DAVID v. GOLIATH

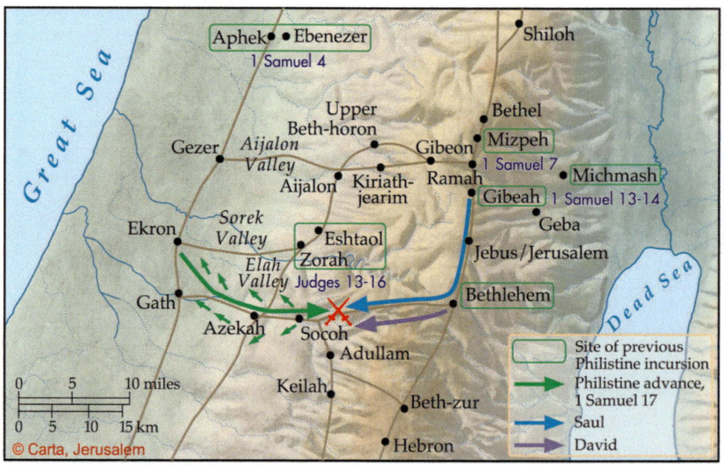

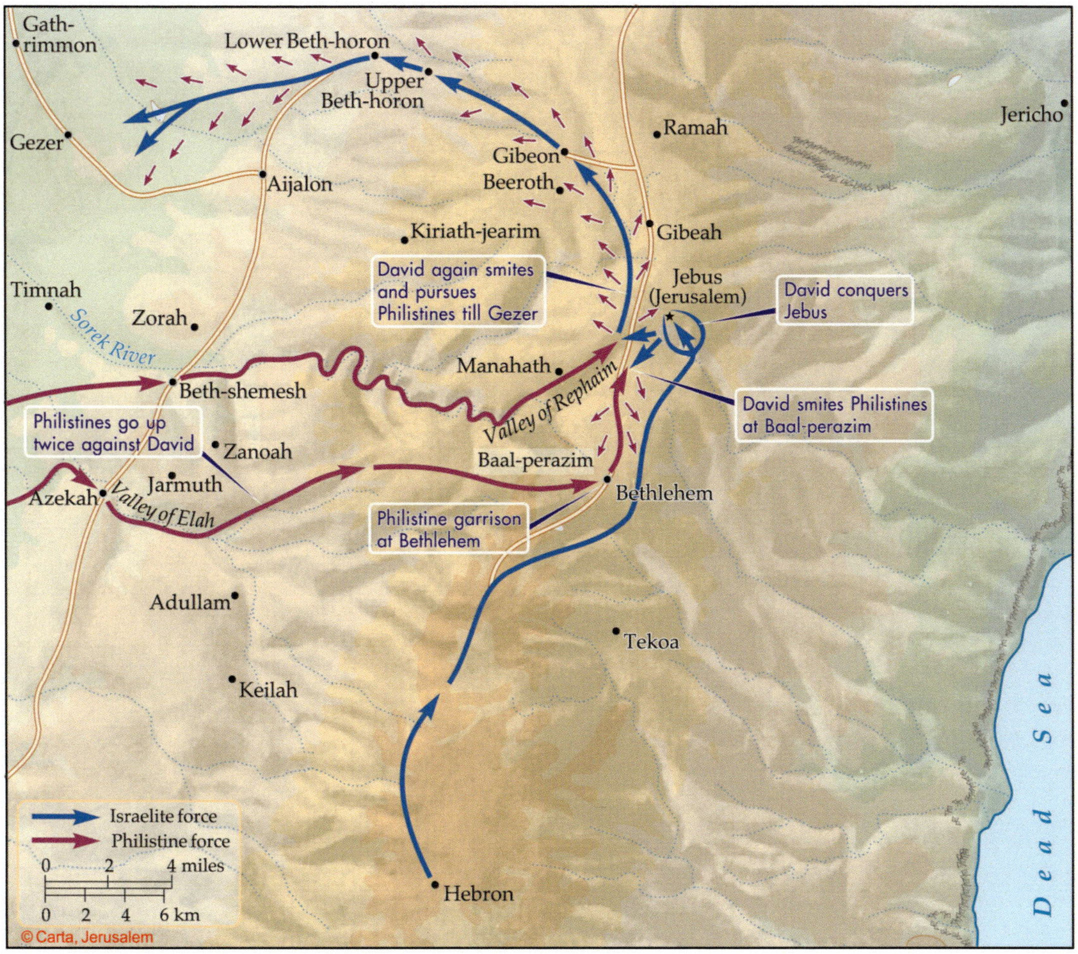

DAVID'S MOVE TO JEBUS (JERUSALEM)

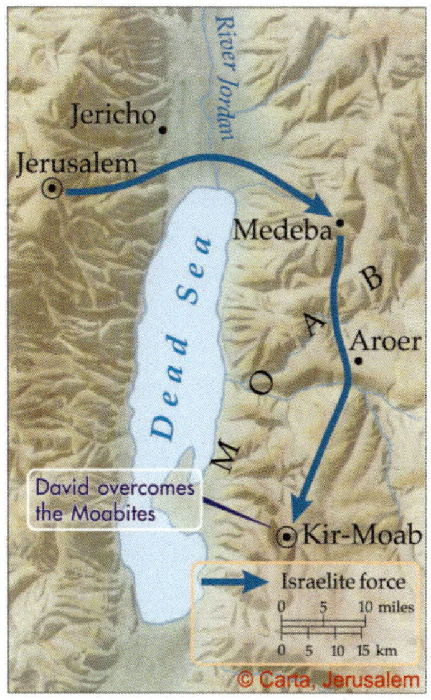

DAVID'S CAMPAIGN AGAINST MOAB

royal line of succession by proclaiming Ish-bosheth (Esh-baal; 1 Chron 8:33), the dead king's son, as king "over Gilead, over the Ashurites, over Jezreel, over Ephraim, and over Benjamin, even over all Israel" (2 Sam 2:8–10). This list of place-names is telling: the house of Saul maintained control over the block of hills on either side of the Jordan River, but the northern tribes (Issachar, Zebulun, Naphtali and Asher), if ever under Saul's command, were gone, as was Judah. David responded by waging a prolonged, and ultimately successful, civil war against the remnants of the house of Saul (2 Sam 2:12–4:12).

One of David's first acts as king of all Israel was to relocate his capital from Hebron to Jerusalem (2 Sam 5:6–9). This was a wise political move on a number of accounts. David realized that Hebron was too far south geographically and too Judean culturally to give him credibility with the tribes in the north. Jerusalem (Jebus) had been allotted to the central tribe of Benjamin (Josh 15:8; 18:16, 28), yet remained a Jebusite (Canaanite) enclave deep in the central hill country. Although Saul's Gibeah lay only five miles north, Israel's first king was unable to, or uninterested in, bringing Jerusalem into the Benjaminite orbit. David redeemed the city and its holdings—thereby gaining favor among the people of Benjamin—but rather than turn Jerusalem over to them he maintained the city's independence, transforming it into a capital for all Israel. The Jebusite fortress had been called the Stronghold of Zion; with its capture, Zion became the City of David, the royal seat of an Israelite national dynasty. Eventually Jerusalem would become one of the world's greatest cities, a city of emotion, song, hope and praise, on the strength of its unique tie to God and the dynasty that He chose to represent His Name on earth (e.g., Psalms 48; 121; 122; 125).

David's move to unite the tribes of Israel at Jerusalem drew a response from Israel's neighbors. Now that David was a *bona fide* player in the southern Levant, Hiram king of Tyre initiated commercial contacts which would eventually result in materials and manpower to build the Jerusalem temple (2 Sam 5:11–12). The Philistines responded to David's conquest of Jerusalem too, but with a show of military force. Twice the Philistines penetrated the rugged hills west of Jerusalem and besieged the new Israelite capital from the Valley of Rephaim (2 Sam 5:17–25; cf. Josh 15:8); twice David flushed them out. With these victories and a follow-up campaign at Gath (2 Sam 8:1; 1 Chron 18:1) David had momentarily removed the Philistine threat. It can be assumed that Philistine control of the northern coastal plain and Jezreel Valley also fell to David, and that Israel was able to subdue old Canaanite urban centers of the region such as Beth-shean, Taanach, Ibleam, Megiddo and Dor in the process (cf. Judg 1:27–28).

David's battles in Transjordan aimed at controlling commercial interests along the King's Highway consumed a significant portion of his reign. While it is difficult to reconstruct the biblical chronology, a probable sequence of events can be suggested based on the overall geographical and political realities that David faced in the east. His first move was against Moab, specifically the Medeba Plateau, former kingdom of Sihon and now home to the Israelite tribe of Reuben (2 Sam 8:2; Num 21:21–32; Deut 2:26–37). David's move posed a threat to Hanun king of the Ammonites, who also needed the plateau as his own front line of expansion. Hanun marshaled support from Beth-rehob, Zobah, Maacah and Tob, emerging Aramean states in northern Transjordan, and engaged David's army east of Medeba, but the Ammonite-Aramean coalition was routed by David's general Joab (2 Sam 10:1–14). David's battles against the Ammonite capital Rabbah, in which Uriah was killed, may have taken place as a follow-up (2 Sam 11:1; 12:26–31). As a consequence, Hadad-ezer king of Zobah pulled together an even larger coalition of Aramean states from as far north as the Euphrates

The morning sun warms the western hills of Moab, revealing the drop of the Kerak wadi toward the Dead Sea. Opposite, in the far distance, rise the hills of the Judean Wilderness toward the Negev and Hebron. The line-of-site connection between Moab and Judah made the relationship between the two peoples impossible to ignore. David's dealings with Moab were complex. His great-grandmother, Ruth, hailed from Moab, and David placed his parents under the protection of the king of Moab while he struggled for ascendancy over Saul (1 Sam 22:3–5). Yet after he became king, David subdued Moab with calculated violence that seems particularly discriminatory (2 Sam 8:2).

to try to stop David from advancing to Damascus. The battle lines were drawn at Helam in eastern Bashan, across the same pivotal land between Israel, Ammon and Aram-Damascus that Moses had taken from Og (Num 21:33–35; Deut 3:1–11). Again, David's forces routed the Arameans, and many members of the coalition became David's vassals (2 Sam 10:15–19). David next took the battle directly to Damascus (2 Sam 8:3–8). Under the Middle Eastern adage "the enemy of my enemy is my friend," Toi king of Hammath, the major Aramean kingdom just north of Damascus and a state always at odds with its southern neighbor, established a treaty of joint-recognition with David (2 Sam 8:9–10), thus surrounding Damascus and bringing the most important Aramean center into David's orbit as a result. At some point David had also defeated Edom in the Valley of Salt, the wasteland of the Rift Valley abutting the southern end of the Dead Sea, and established garrisons throughout that land as well (1 Kgs 11:14–22).

David was perhaps less successful in domestic matters. Problems of tribal unification still loomed large, and he took various steps to try to bring all Israel together. He allowed Mephibosheth, Saul's lame son and the last hope of his truncated dynasty, for instance, to "eat at the king's table," thereby bestowing status and honor on the remnants of Saul's line and hopefully gaining northern loyalty in the process (2 Sam 9:1–13; cf. 4:4). And of course David brought the Ark of the Covenant from Kiriath-jearim—it had lacked a proper home since the Philistines had destroyed Shiloh during the days of Eli and Samuel—to Jerusalem with an eye toward establishing Jerusalem as the primary religious center of the country (2 Sam 6:1–23; 7:1–29). Yet rebellion was always at hand, even in his own family. Typical to monarchies in the ancient Near East, David had multiple wives, partly to cement diplomatic relations with neighboring states and partly as a sign of wealth and prestige. And, true to form, sons from some of his lesser queens actively positioned themselves for the throne. Of note are Absalom, whose *coup d'état* was nearly successful, and Adonijah (2 Sam 15:1–18:18), who jumped the secession gun by attempting to have himself crowned king while David was on his deathbed (1 Kgs 1:5–53; 2:19–25).

David's nominal control of the entire Levant, from the Sinai to the Euphrates River, was consistent with the covenant that God had made with Abraham: "To your descendants I have given this land, from the river of Egypt as far as the great river, the River Euphrates" (cf. 1 Kgs 4:21; cf. Gen 15:18). Moreover, the genuine remorse that David showed in response to the Bathsheba Affair is not only a timeless example of true repentance, but shows that this king was different than the others and worthy of launching a very special kingdom (2 Sam 11:1–12:25; Ps 51:1–19). And David's relationship with the prophet Nathan was both personal and far-reaching, establishing a protocol that could have guided the relationship between Israel's king and temple in future generations.

David died in peace (1 Kgs 2:1–12), yet nothing was so secure that the future of the kingdom could be assured. In some ways the tasks that faced Solomon, eldest living son of the great royal queen, Bathsheba, were even greater than his father's, for loyalties could not be assumed and the young monarch's own hands had not been hardened in battle. Moreover, a rich son in the public eye too often succumbs to the playboy syndrome, and Solomon had certain tendencies that had to be refined. Because a new nation is most at risk during its first transfer of power, Solomon had to show decisive leadership or David's legacy would have been in vain. By removing any hint of insurrection among those close to the throne, including David's priest Abiathar and general Joab, both of whom had supported the usurper Adonijah, and Shimei, a holdover from the house of Saul (1 Kgs 2:5–6, 19–46), Solomon gained the necessary reputation to hold onto a kingdom in a part of the world where strength is respected and a show of weakness always exploited.

The focal point of Solomon's kingdom was the city of Jerusalem, where two magnificent new buildings were constructed. These were the royal palace and temple, each representing one of the two primary institutions of the state. Although no certain archaeological remains of either have been found,[14] it is likely that the palace would have been at the northern, higher and more secure end of the city where Solomon could have full view of his subjects (and they of him), and the temple above (north of) that. These were built with the help of Hiram, king of Tyre, who provided the necessary construction materials, workmen and expertise to do the job, thereby reestablishing the economic treaty that he had established with David (1 Kgs 5:1–12; cf. 2 Sam 5:11–12). Both buildings incorporated north Syrian and Egyptian designs and motifs,[15] and reflected nicely Solomon's growing status in the ancient Near East. Of course, the temple was first and foremost a place worthy of the presence of the LORD God, and its architectural and artistic elements portrayed God's interaction with His people at creation and on Mt. Sinai while al-

THE JERUSALEM OF DAVID AND SOLOMON

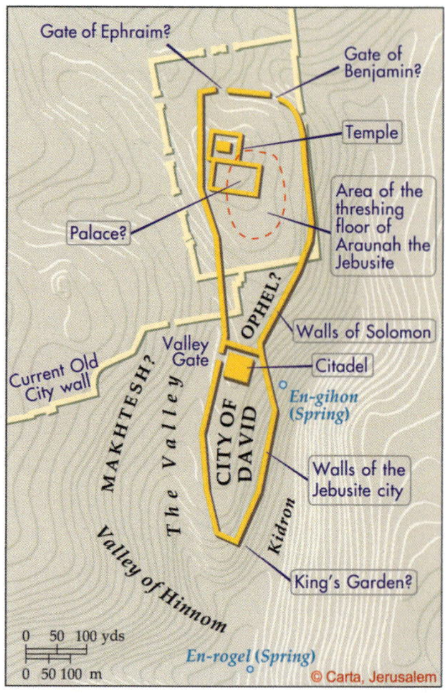

SOLOMON'S BUILDING PROJECTS

lowing the Israelites to publicly express their ongoing covenantal relationship with Him. The temple was dedicated in a fantastic ceremony in which Solomon bound himself and his people to God, and blessed and thanked God for fulfilling the promises He had made to Abraham, Moses and David (1 Kgs 8:1–66).

Solomon acknowledged that it would take all the wisdom that he could muster (and God could give) to govern his kingdom in ways that benefited his people (1 Kgs 3:3–15; 9:1–9). Problems facing families and individuals, such as that of the two women with one live baby (1 Kgs 3:16–28), were always at hand. More intractable were those that had the potential to tear at the entire social fabric of the kingdom, such as the ongoing need to foster tribal unity and the dilemma of how to incorporate indigenous Canaanite elements still found in the land under the Israelite umbrella. The list of Solomon's twelve district governors (1 Kgs 4:7–19) indicates that the new national administration respected the old tribal boundaries, while incorporating the Canaanite lowlands conquered by David into new districts.[16] In this way Solomon struck a balance between the expediency of allowing established tribes to maintain their individual identities, and the necessity of binding everyone to the good of the kingdom. While each of the districts was responsible for sending the equivalent of one month's supply of foodstuffs and provisions to the "king's table" (taxes to support the royal bureaucracy; 1 Kgs 4:21–28) and providing corvée workers for royal projects (1 Kgs 5:13–18; 9:15, 17–23), the people of the land were generally satisfied, each living "under his own vine and his fig tree" (1 Kgs 4:20, 25). It's a picture of "the good life" such as a typical 10th century B.C. Israelite could hope to gain, with everyone rejoicing in God and king and secure in their station in life.

David had forged political alliances throughout the Levant, alliances that Solomon reaffirmed with a series of royal marriages and sealed by building shrines in Jerusalem dedicated to his wives' homeland deities (1 Kgs 11:1–8). Foremost among these was a treaty with Egypt (the Pharaoh was likely Siamun), sealed by diplomatic marriage and evidenced by Solomon's rights to the city of Gezer, Jerusalem's gateway to the international priorities of the coast (1 Kgs 9:16). By fortifying Gezer, Megiddo and Hazor Solomon was able to exert Israelite control over the international economy north and west, while by building Tamar in the Wilderness (*En Hazeva*) he could control routes south and east, to the port of Ezion-geber on the Red Sea and beyond (1 Kgs 9:15–18, 26–28). Solomon was now in position to become the major economic player in the Levant, tying together routes and markets that stretched from Egypt and Arabia to Kue (Cilicia) and dealing in the expensive commodities of the day such as horses and chariots (1 Kgs 10:28–29). In a visit reminiscent of that of the Queen of Punt to Hatshepsut in the early 15th century B.C. (recorded in pictures on Hatshepsut's funerary temple at Deir el-Bahri in Upper Egypt), the Queen of Sheba (a land found either in today's Yemen or Somalia) made a call on Solomon and was duly impressed with what he had accomplished (1 Kgs 10:1–13).

Solomon stands in the tradition of great men of state who had the time and opportunity to turn their talents to more refined pursuits, renaissance men like Ashurbanipal, Ptolemy II Philadelphus and Thomas Jefferson who engaged in science (as it was known), literature and the arts. Solomon is best known for his wisdom, which he was more successful expressing in the form of proverbs, poetry and song (1 Kgs 4:29–34; Proverbs 1–29; Song of Songs; Psalm 72) than by his own actions.

In the end, Solomon's lifestyle—and other factors—caught up with him. The writer of Kings roundly condemned Solomon for making concessions to the gods of his foreign wives, thereby tainting the unique call of God on Israel (1 Kgs 11:1–13). But this was just one aspect of the deep-seated social and economic unrest that had never stopped tearing at the underbelly of his kingdom. Eventually the extraordinary effort that it took to keep the country together from the top was overwhelmed by any number of factors down the line, some within the government, some among the masses, some at the borders. The economy was propelled partly by revenue from vassals and trade, and partly by taxation. It was the latter that seemed particularly unjust to the still-independent-minded northern tribes and prompted their revolt soon after Solomon died and the kingdom passed to his son, Rehoboam (1 Kgs 12:1–20). Expecting that one day the façade of Solomon's kingdom would crack, Pharaoh Shishak, who had patronized Jeroboam (1 Kgs 11:26–40), attacked in Rehoboam's fifth year, slicing through the weakened Levant and reducing Israel and Judah to two hollow shells (1 Kgs 14:25–26; 2 Chron 12:1–12; cf. 2 Chron 11:5–12). The United Kingdom of David and Solomon collapsed into rump states as truncated as the kingdom had been at the death of Saul. Israel's golden age ended with the realization that the very best efforts of the most talented leaders is never quite enough in the end. For the biblical writers, David became an image of what yet could someday be, while real hope for the future rested on the belief that a son of David, one who was truly anointed (*messiah*), would someday arise to instill Davidic greatness in all God's people (Isa 55:3; Jer 30:9; Ezek 37:24–28; Zech 12:8, 10; Mt 1:1; Lk 2:11).

AHAB AND JEHOSHAPHAT

Ahab took the throne of the Northern Kingdom of Israel in 874 B.C., fifty-seven years after the death of Solomon, and Jehoshaphat began his reign over Judah, after a two-year co-regency with his father Asa, four years later (1 Kgs 15:24; 16:29; 22:51; 2 Chron 20:31). As two men who were roughly the same age, Ahab and Jehoshaphat were comrades, and rivals. Both tried to reestablish a bit of the glory days of Solomon on their own side of a shared border, and were largely successful, though in very different ways, in the effort.

The years following the split of Solomon's kingdom were a traumatic time for Judah and Israel. Pharaoh Shishak's run through the southern Levant had left Israel and Judah staggering (1 Kgs 14:25–26; 2 Chron 12:1–12). Redirecting their efforts inward, the next several decades saw both states fighting over the territory of Benjamin, their own land between (1 Kgs 15:16, 32; 2 Chron 13:1–19). Skirmishes on the Benjamin plateau north of Jerusalem, a crossroads more vital to Judah than Israel, eventually brought the region under the control of Asa, the father of Jehoshaphat (1 Kgs 15:17–22). Israel meanwhile was engaged in a prolonged struggle to take Gibbethon, just west of Gezer, in an attempt to check Judah's aspirations on the coast. The scene was a maker and breaker of dynasties, as two generals commanding the fight at Gibbethon, Baasha and then Omri, each used their success on the battlefield to seize the Israelite throne (1 Kgs 15:27–33; 16:15–20).

Omri's rule was not accepted by everyone, and it took nearly six years of civil war for his army to control all Israel (1 Kgs 16:21–23). But with his full accession to the throne, the kingdom's fortunes took a noticeable step forward. Omri's dynasty (Israel's third, not counting the aborted reign of Zimri) gained so much international attention that Jehu, who would eventually overthrow Omri's royal house in 841 B.C., was nevertheless called "Jehu son of Omri," and the northern kingdom itself "the house of Omri," in Assyrian texts.[17]

In his six undisputed years as king (880–874 B.C.), Omri laid a strong foundation for Israel to reestablish itself as a major player in the southern Levant. One of his most important acts was to move the location of the Israelite capital from Tirzah, a city tucked in the eastern hills of Manasseh with good access only to the Jordan Valley and Transjordan, to Samaria, facing the coast (1 Kgs 16:24; cf. 12:25; 14:17; 15:21; 16:8–9, 23). For Omri, a capital that served only the regional needs of an inland kingdom was clearly insufficient, and Samaria symbolized but also facilitated his goal of reestablishing ties with the commercial outlets of Phoenicia. Although Ahab gets the credit (or blame), it was certainly Omri who arranged the marriage of his son to Jezebel, daughter of the Phoenician king, in a diplomatic formality that sealed the renewal of a political and economic reality that had defined the kingdom of Solomon (1 Kgs 16:31). But Omri also needed raw materials to push through the ports of Phoenicia and so turned east, to the tableland of Medeba which the king of Moab had meanwhile seized from Israel after the death of Solomon. By pushing Moab back and reestablishing a fortified Israelite presence in Transjordan, Omri and his son Ahab were able to profit as middlemen in the delivery of sheep and ram's wool from Moab to the Phoenicians. It was the latter who, in addition to controlling the sea lanes, had a monopoly on red-purple dye and trade in fine garments (2 Kgs 3:4; cf. Ezek 27:7).[18] In order to make sure that the route between Moab and the coast would pass through Israel, Hiel from Bethel rebuilt Jericho, Israel's southeastern gateway, early in the reign of Ahab (1 Kgs 16:34). As a result, Judah's access to the east around the northern end of the Dead Sea was hindered, forcing Jehoshaphat to concentrate on the difficult but potentially more lucrative southeastern routes into Edom instead.

THE BATTLE FOR BENJAMIN

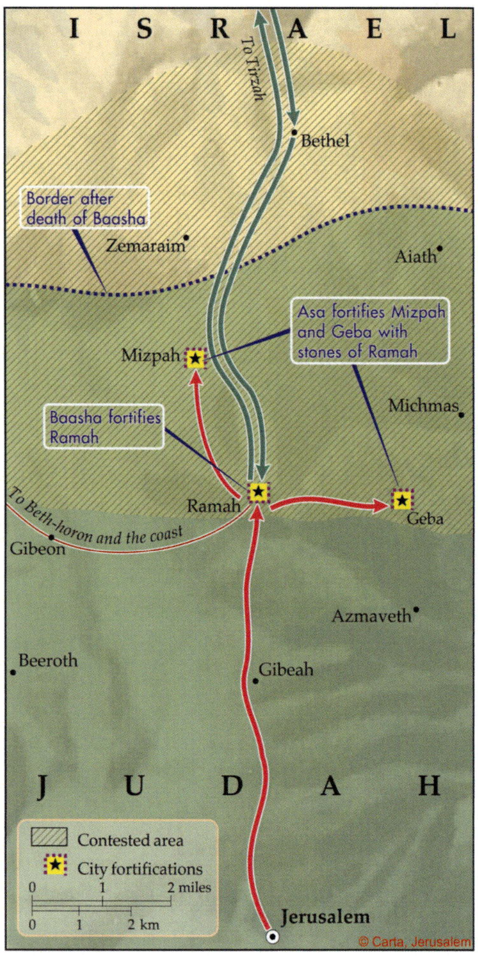

While Omri and Ahab had to use their hardscrabble genes to build a kingdom, Jehoshaphat, a conventional man, inherited his. The long reign of Jehoshaphat's father, Asa (911–870 B.C.), had brought stability to the throne in the south just when the northern kingdom was churning out one *coup d'état* after another, and with it came initial success on the battlefield (1 Kgs 15:16–22; 2 Chron 14:8–15). Moreover, Asa fostered a religious conservatism that gave priority to the LORD as the proper God of Judah, over against certain tolerant, internationalizing elements of Judah's population that paid homage to other deities (2 Chron 15:8–19). The northern kings never seemed to be too bothered by such issues. According to the writers of Kings and Chronicles, the kings of the south who were most successful in matters of religion (i.e., devotion to the LORD and His temple in Jerusalem) were also the most successful in politics (fostering a secure, stable society and promoting a favorable international policy). Asa, on the balance, was one of these, and his son Jehoshaphat learned the role well. Grounded in a solid dynasty, Jehoshaphat was born to a sense of duty and understood the need to foster first the welfare his kingdom's people.

Ahab inherited rights to the coast through Omri's alliance with Phoenicia, and continued his father's policy of control over Moab. With these bases intact, he turned his attention to the Arameans, a perennial threat to Israel's goal of dominating the King's Highway in Transjordan. The only way that Ahab could concentrate on things northeast, however, was by formalizing a truce in the south, with Judah. This easing of relations with Jerusalem was sealed with the marriage of Ahab's daughter, Athaliah, to Jehoram, son of Jehoshaphat and crown prince of Judah (2 Kgs 8:16–18, 25–27). The Israel-Judah alliance allowed the respite needed for each nation to expand their respective spheres of influence over parts of the southern Levant. Echoes of the once-unified kingdom of David and Solomon could be heard.

Athaliah, like Jezebel, was a strong personality and seems to have been a dominant player in affairs of state in Judah, constantly reminding Jehoshaphat that he lived under the shadow of her daddy, his stronger and more politically ambitious neighbor

THE CAPITALS OF ISRAEL

This was Ahab's eastward view from his palace at Jezreel, down the Harod Valley toward Transjordan. The northern slope of Mount Gilboa, where Saul and Jonathan lost their lives in battle with the Philistines, rises on the right. The term Jezreel Valley must have referred originally to these flat lands at the base of the mound of Jezreel. Ahab used Jezreel as a chariot base to control international traffic in the Jezreel Valley corridor and to launch attacks along his border with Aram-Damascus.

to the north. Like Jezebel, Athaliah outlived her husband, even becoming for a time sole ruler in the land (queen by proxy, so to say; 2 Kgs 11:1–16; 2 Chron 22:1–23:15). For the writers of Kings and Chronicles, however, Athaliah's similarity to Jezebel lay in her role as a queen of Baal and Asherah. Both women, they insisted, undermined the true strength of Israel and Judah, nations which had been founded on the Kingship of the LORD God, and for this they were condemned.

Ahab based his moves against Damascus from Jezreel, a large rectangular fortress that served as a royal chariot base at the edge of the Jezreel Valley (cf. 2 Kgs 9:17, 31–32; 10:8). As a point-counterpoint to the king's military ambitions, the only events that the Bible mentions as having taken place in Jezreel during the reign of Ahab focus on Elijah, his prophetic nemesis (1 Kgs 18:45–46), and Naboth, whom Ahab murdered and despoiled (1 Kgs 21:1–29). Fittingly, it was at Jezreel that the house of Omri was eventually overthrown and the aging queen mother, Jezebel, assassinated (2 Kgs 9:14–37).

Much of Ahab's reign was taken up by fights with the Damascus-based Arameans. The sequence of battlegrounds was first Samaria (in 857 B.C.; 1 Kings 20:1–21), then Aphek east of the Sea of Galilee, on more neutral ground (856 B.C.; 1 Kgs 20:22–34). In both cases Ahab prevailed, but then everything gave way to a flow of larger events. Assyrian storm clouds loomed on the northern horizon, the beginning stages of what would become two hundred years of "calculated frightfulness" (in the words of the Assyriologist A. T. Olmstead[19]) aimed at Egypt and the west. In anticipation, the short period between 856 and 853 B.C. saw a measure of cooperation (forced or otherwise) between the kingdoms of the southern Levant, resulting in a degree of prosperity for Israel and Judah that had not been seen since the days of Solomon. Israel's old landed aristocracy—tribal, clan and city elders—largely fell in line behind their powerful and charismatic leader (1 Kgs 20:13–14; 21:8–13). To cover his bases, Ahab surrounded himself with a loyal band of prophets who were quick to soothe his conscience and ensure that the will of the gods would bend his way (cf. 1 Kgs 22:6). Throughout, the prophet Elijah had been taking orders from a different King, prompting the strong-willed and often exasperated Ahab to label him "troubler of Israel" (1 Kgs 18:17).

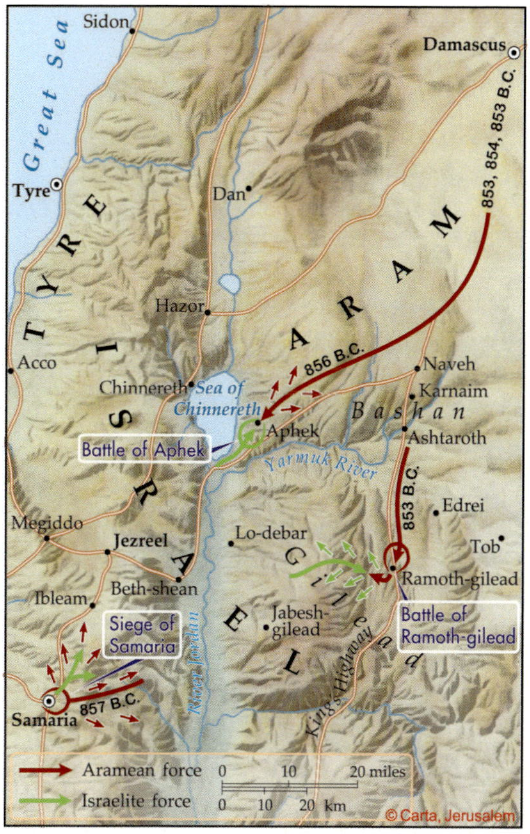

AHAB'S WARS WITH ARAM, 857–853 B.C.

THE BATTLE OF QARQAR

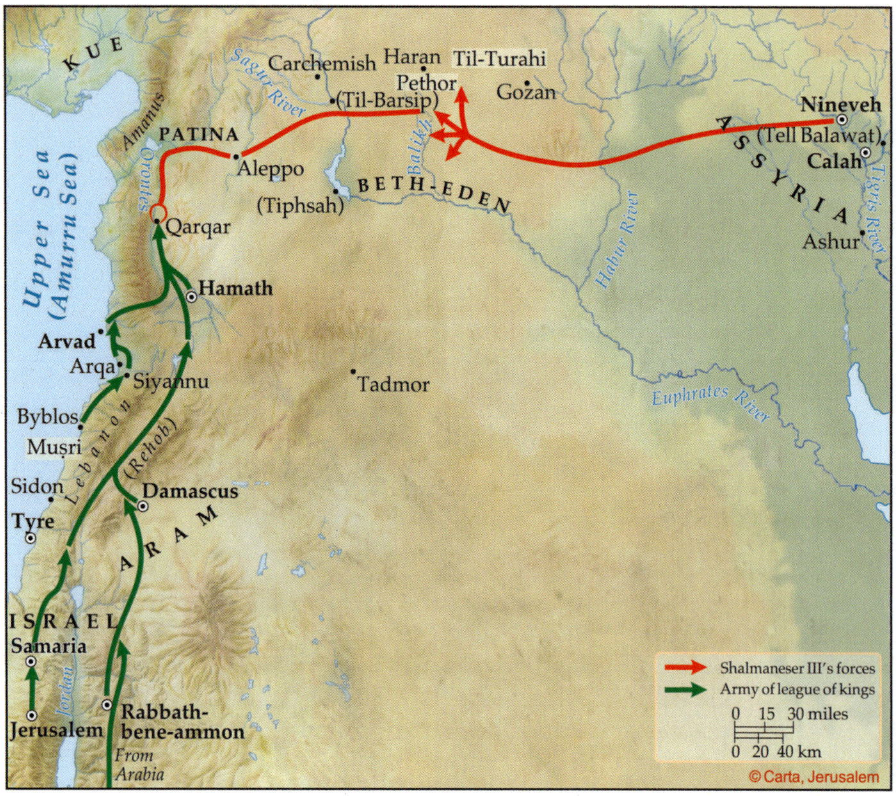

The truce lasted three years (1 Kgs 22:1). In 853 B.C. the Assyrian king Shalmaneser III crossed the Euphrates near the old patriarchal city of Haran, smashed through Aleppo and drew his battle line against the Arameans at Qarqar on the Orontes in the northern Levant. Realizing that everyone in the Assyrian path stood to lose alike, the kingdoms of the Levant plus Egypt and Arabia formed a formal coalition to stop Shalmaneser. An Assyrian source shows that the coalition was led by the king of Aram-Damascus, the king of Hamath and by Ahab.[20] In it the king of Israel is listed as commanding the largest chariot force. Though Shalmaneser claimed a resounding victory, it is apparent that the coalition held the line.

Buoyed by his role at Qarqar, Ahab followed up by breaking the coalition and taking the offense against the Arameans. In rash confidence, he pushed the site of confrontation all the way out to Ramoth-gilead, an easy chariot ride from Damascus. Ahab sought the support of Judah, and Jehoshaphat, the junior partner, willingly agreed (1 Kgs 22:1–4). It was a decisive moment: Jehoshaphat survived, but Ahab was killed in the chaos of battle and the coalition troops fled, defeated (1 Kgs 22:29–40).

Only a few months had passed since the great battlefield success at Qarqar, yet now, with the death of Ahab, everything had changed. Ahab was succeeded by two of his sons, Ahaziah (853–852 B.C.) and then Jehoram (852–841 B.C.), neither of whom inherited a full measure of their father's skills (1 Kgs 22:51–53; 2 Kgs 1:1–18; 3:1). Aram-Damascus was certainly strengthened, and although Israel would continue to fight for control of Ramoth-gilead for another twelve years (2 Kgs 8:28; 9:14–15), the remainder of the ninth century B.C. saw the Aramean kings pretty much have their way with Israel (cf. 2 Kgs 13:7; Amos 1:3). Mesha king of Moab, too, seized the moment, throwing off the hated Israelite yoke and reclaiming the Medeba Plateau (cf. 2 Kgs 1:1; 3:4–5).[21]

And as for the king of Judah—he could finally be his own man. Jehoshaphat's skills and abilities, until now somewhat latent and subservient to Ahab, suddenly had the freedom to develop and mature. Judah no doubt had enjoyed a measure of prosperity that came hand-in-hand with the success of Ahab (2 Chron 18:1), but according to the sequence of events recorded in Chronicles—and there is a certain cause-and-effect logic to its flow—it was only after Jehoshaphat witnessed the violent death of Ahab that the Judean king realized the priority of fostering a religious-nationalistic revival in his land, centered on the will of the LORD God (2 Chron 19:1–4).

Jehoshaphat appointed a line of judges to serve in the fortified cities of Judah, and designated priests, Levites and high-level officials (a sort of court of last resort) in Jerusalem in an attempt to centralize and enforce a single standard of justice throughout the kingdom (2 Chron 19:5–11). Perhaps the king was motivated to save Judah the excesses of social and economic injustice that had taken root in Israel under the patronage of Ahab, or maybe he simply wanted to strengthen his rule from the top down. In any case, Jehoshaphat's success in the face of the honored line of village elders—dispensers of justice from time immemorial—and in spite of the influence of Athaliah toward things of Ahab, is admirable, and can be credited to the stable relationship that the people of Judah had with their ruling dynasty as well as the personality of Jehoshaphat himself. Much of Judah's prosperity came from Jehoshaphat's control of the southern trade routes, especially the movement of exotic goods from Arabia and the Red Sea to Philistia and ports on the Mediterranean (2 Chron 17:10–13; cf. 1 Kgs 22:48–49; 2 Chron 20:35–37). To strengthen his hold on these lucrative markets, Jehoshaphat replaced the king of Edom with a governor loyal to Judah (1 Kgs 22:47). And he twice checked Moabite advances in fights that were possible only because Ahab was off the scene (2 Kgs 3:6–27; 2 Chron 20:1–25).

Jehoshaphat died five years after Ahab, in 848 B.C. His legacy did not survive him. In a story that smacks of the behavior of the northern kings, Jehoram, the husband of Ahab's daughter Athaliah, purged the Judean royal household in fear of internal threats (2 Chron 21:4), then faced open rebellion on every frontier (2 Kgs 8:20–23; 2 Chron 21:8–17). By the time he died in 841 B.C., Judah's holdings in land and capital had been gutted. Within months his son Ahaziah was assassinated, along with Ahab's grandson, Jehoram of Israel, at Jezreel by the Israelite general Jehu (2 Kgs 9:27–29). The old queen mother Jezebel met her fate, too. Hearing that Jehu had seized the throne, she "painted her eyes, adorned her head and looked out the window" of her upper chambers—from which she was promptly thrown to her death (2 Kgs 9:30–37). At least the old gal went out in style. The dynasty of Omri had ended; that of David and Solomon barely survived. For better or worse, a new age had dawned in Israel and Judah.

The writer of Kings emphasized the deeds of Ahab, while the post-exilic Chronicler, concerned with the reestablishment of the nation of Judah, naturally focused on Jehoshaphat. Both writers judged human events by how closely their participants—especially the kings of Israel and Judah—adhered to the commands and expectations of the LORD God. While this is a common theme throughout the Bible, it is perhaps most pronounced for the events of the ninth century B.C. as Israel and Judah, left largely alone by the world powers, sought to establish patterns of national behavior that were favorable for their own interests. The prophetic voice, nearly drowned out by Ahab, was better heard by Jehoshaphat, and the biblical writers made a point to note that whatever was left of justice, righteousness and common decency among the people of the land, could be still be found in Judah.

ISAIAH

Isaiah's mission as a prophet to Judah coincided with the arrival of the Assyrians in the southern Levant. He witnessed Tiglath-pileser III's three quick thrusts (to the coastal plain, to Galilee and to Transjordan) in 734–732 B.C. (cf. Isa 9:1), looked in horror as the northern kingdom of Israel fell to Shalmaneser V (722 B.C.) and as Sargon II pushed through Philistia (720, 713 and 712 B.C.), and survived Sennacherib's assault on Judah and Jerusalem in 701 B.C. It was nothing but trouble for king and people alike as the Assyrian flood came "up to the neck" of Judah (Isa 8:8).

But if this were all that the people of Judah had to face, their spiritual and moral backbone could have seen them through. The real tragedy lay not so much in the devastation of the Assyrian attack as in the fact that Judah was already so shot through with moral failings that the social fabric of society was fatally wounded before Tiglath-pileser even arrived. With a mind that penetrated to the real problem, Isaiah spent most of his time blasting his own people—then picking up the pieces. This was an unpopular task and certainly one that was not politically correct. It took a special kind of person to stand in the gap, and with God's help Isaiah proved equal to the challenge at hand.

The first part of the Book of Isaiah (chapters 1–39) is framed by accounts of Isaiah's interaction with two of Judah's kings, Ahaz and Hezekiah. Each encounter is set in the context of a military attack on Judah, the first by Aram-Damascus and Israel in 735 B.C. in anticipation of Tiglath-pileser's dramatic entrance into the land (Isa 7:1–9:7), and the second by Sennacherib in 701 B.C. (Isa 36:1–39:8). The latter part of the Book of Isaiah (chapters 40–66), a glorious, sweeping view of Israel's future, is as much a reflection of the need for hope during troubled times as it is a picture of what would some day be. There is a long-standing discussion in scholarly circles as to the suitability of using these chapters to understand the late eighth century B.C. prophet, although the present, canonical shape of the book does encourage a holistic reading.[22] In any case, when read together, the disparate parts of the Book of Isaiah provide a vibrant picture of the man for whom the book is named and the greatness of one whose vision was grounded in the reality of a God who controlled past, present and future. The greatness of Isaiah (both the person and the book) lay in his ability to pierce the blackness of the moment and see that not only was a great light shining somewhere behind the dark cloud that had enveloped everything (Isa 9:2), but that that light, the glory of the LORD himself, would someday allow his people to "arise, shine… see and be radiant" (Isa 60:1, 5).

Isaiah was apparently a native of Jerusalem, an advisor and confidant to the Judean royal court as and perhaps even related to it by marriage (a tradition mentioned by the Babylonian Talmud notes that Isaiah's father Amoz was a brother of King Uzziah[23]). Isaiah's prophetic ministry began sometime late in the reign of Uzziah (767–740 B.C.), spanned the reigns of Jotham (740–732 B.C.), Ahaz (732–716 B.C.) and Hezekiah (716–687 B.C.), and most probably extended into the early part of the reign of Manasseh since he reported the death of Sennacherib which happened in 681 B.C. (Isa 1:1; 37:38). He was married, with children (Isa 7:3; 8:3), and literate, probably trained as a scribe (Isa 8:1). Though an urbanite, Isaiah was also at home in the countryside, out and about in the hills and valleys of Judah and Israel. This we can assume, for his vividly descriptive prophetic imagery was energized by an intimate knowledge of land and nature, trees, grass and flowers, and animals, birds and insects (e.g., Isa 5:1–7; 28:24–28; 30:6; 34:13–15). Isaiah likely owned fields and orchards somewhere in the environs of Jerusalem. On the pattern of Amos (Amos 1:1; 7:14), Elisha (1 Kgs 19:19) and Jesus (Mt 13:55) he probably also had marketable skills and, by extension, personal experience in business matters, assumed by his keen awareness of issues of interpersonal propriety and what makes for justice and righteousness on the street.

Isaiah's prophetic ministry took on a fresh intensity "in the year that king Uzziah died" (Isa 6:1). With Assyria in a temporary cycle of decline, Uzziah had steered his kingdom through a period of prosperity and growth, exerting his influence as far as both the Mediterranean and Red seas (2 Kgs 14:22; 2 Chron 26:6–15). Assyrian records even suggest that Uzziah (there called Azriyau/Azariah) led a coalition of south Levantine states against Tiglath-pileser III (named Pul by the writer of Kings) in the region of Hamath in 743 B.C., temporarily checking this first of the renewed Assyrian attacks in the region (cf. 2 Kgs 15:19–20).[24]

THE CAMPAIGNS OF UZZIAH

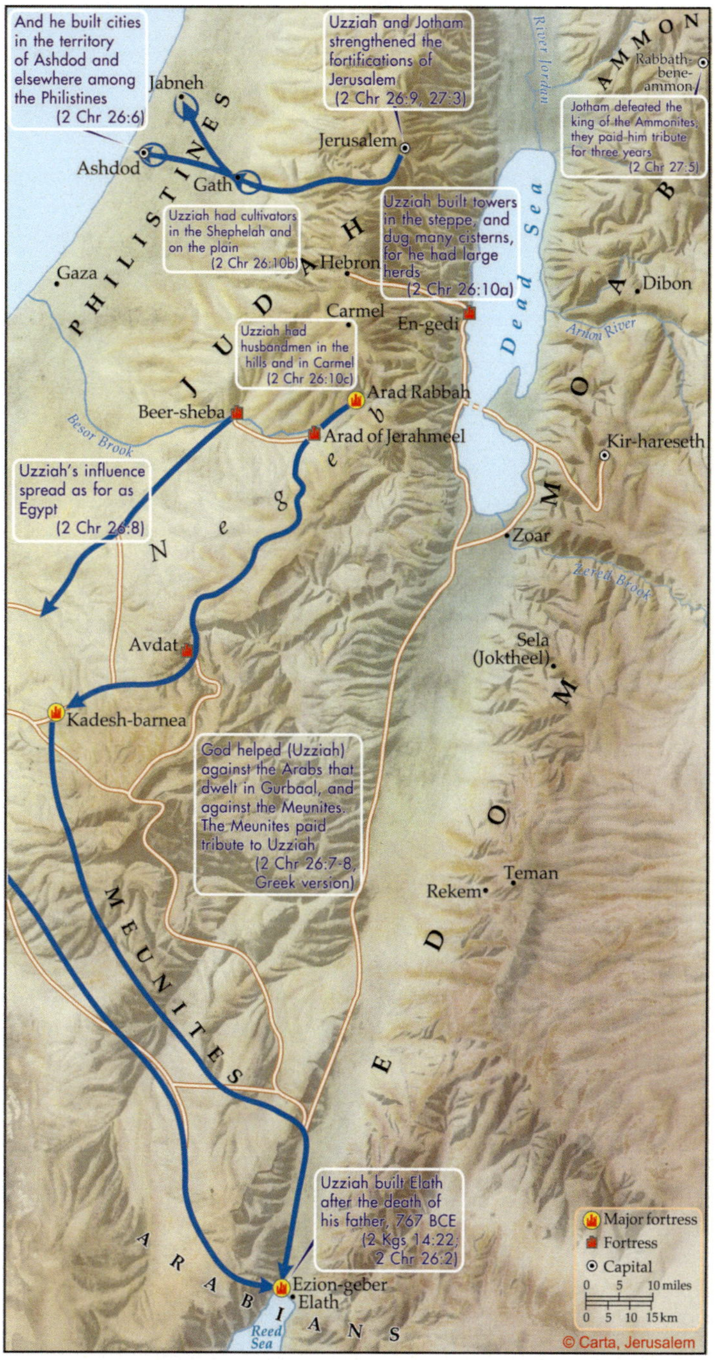

THE CAMPAIGNS OF TIGLATH-PILESER III, 734–732 B.C.

But Uzziah died just as Assyria again reared its head above the northeastern horizon (2 Chron 26:16–23). The timing could not have been more ominous, and sometime during that year Isaiah, still a young man, had a vivid and dramatic encounter with the LORD (Isa 6:1–7). The setting, God's throne room in the Jerusalem temple, was one of intense majesty. Overcome with the realization of his own inadequacy and failings, Isaiah received divine assurance that his sins were forgiven. Then came the nearly impossible commission: the prophet was to tell his people that in spite of the obvious economic, political and military strength of their nation, they were about to be invaded by the most feared and efficient war machine the world had yet known, and lacked the moral and spiritual fiber necessary to find a way to survive (Isa 6:8–13).

Fortunately for Judah, Uzziah's son, Jotham, followed in his father's footsteps, with policies that can be best described as anti-Assyrian. But the tide was turning. Israel's old nemesis to the northeast, Aram-Damascus, saw in Uzziah's death a chance to restore its control over the trade routes of Transjordan, while the Northern Kingdom of Israel also tried to revive their own interests there. At the same time, Tiglath-pileser III advanced into north Syria, annexing to the Assyrian Empire nineteen political districts around Hamath up to the very doorstep of Aram-Damascus. Assyria's long-term goal was to conquer Egypt, and everything that lay in the way, including Israel and Judah, either had to capitulate or be eaten up.

For the nation states of the southern Levant, it was time for action. In league together, Pekah king of Israel and Rezin king of Damascus turned against Judah, the first overture of the so-called "Syro-Ephramite War." Both wanted the Judean king to join their coalition against the Assyrians. Sensing trouble, a party of pro-Assyrian supporters in Jerusalem deposed Jotham in 735 B.C. and placed his son Ahaz on the throne. Ahaz was a relist who felt that it was better just to cooperate with Assyria. For the kings of Israel and Aram-Damascus, Judah's pro-Assyria shift in foreign policy was tantamount to international treachery. They immediately attacked Jerusalem, intent on subduing the city and replacing Ahaz—and the dynasty of David—with an unnamed "son of Tabeel" who had the guts (or foolishness) to stand up to the Assyrian king (2 Kgs 16:5; Isa 7:1-2, 6). Then in stepped Isaiah, a man who loved both God and country. Isaiah was no fan of Ahaz's pro-Assyrian policy, yet respected both the office of king as well as the descendant of David who filled the throne at any given moment. Under the instruction of the LORD, Isaiah met Ahaz as the latter was on his rounds inspecting the infrastructure of the city and counseled a cautious, stay-put approach: this local threat, Isaiah said, was just that, and would soon be swept away by the floodtide of Assyria anyway (Isa 7:3-9; 8:1-7). Then came the scary part: Isaiah warned Ahaz that Assyria would nearly swallow up Judah as well—the king's pro-Assyrian leanings would do nothing to prevent that—but offered hope that his kingdom would survive in spite of his reckless policies (Isa 7:17-25; 8:8).

Over the next three years, from 734-732 B.C., Tiglath-pileser III attacked, conquered and annexed the northern coastal plain, all of Galilee, Damascus and northern Transjordan, killing Rezin and reducing the northern kingdom of Israel to a clipped state isolated in the hills of Ephraim and Manasseh (2 Kgs 15:29).[25] Through it all Ahaz had hoped to buy Assyria's favor by paying a sizable tribute to Tiglath-pileser and trying to act like a good Assyrian in the process (cf. 2 Kgs 16:10-16). Tiglath-pileser, glad that the tribute he would have taken anyway came so easily, didn't need Judah's help and in the process reduced Ahaz' shrinking kingdom to vassal status (2 Chron 28:19-21).

So much for the historical context of our record of Isaiah's first run-in with a king of Judah. What is often tragically overlooked when offering an account of the sweep of battles and kings is the personal devastation that is foisted on the mass of common people beneath. But they were not out of Isaiah's vision, which, to borrow the words of Abraham Haschel, "felt fiercely"[26] (Isa 7:19-25; 8:9, 21). Lives would be shattered, indeed, not because of the Assyrians *per se*, but because the Judeans deserved it (Isa 1:1-31). Isaiah's path of hope was both simple and profound: *Immanu-el*, "God is with us" (Isa 7:14; 8:8, 10).

When Tiglath-pileser died in 727 B.C., his successor Shalmaneser V renewed the Assyrian push to Egypt. The truncated kingdom of Israel was next in line to be gobbled up (2 Kgs 17:4-6). The siege of Samaria, Israel's capital, lasted three grueling years, time enough for many Israelites to flee south into Judah, refugees under the protection of Ahaz and later his son Hezekiah. Archaeological evidence suggests that the higher, broad hill that today is part of Jerusalem's Jewish and Armenian Quarters and the so-called Mt. Zion hill outside of the current city walls became densely settled in the latter part of the eighth century B.C.,[27] and it is tempting to correlate this sudden expansion with the influx of Israelite refugees. In any case, Isaiah's Jerusalem was a growing city and its kings, Ahaz and then Hezekiah (in 715 B.C.), became fully embroiled in international affairs. Isaiah, with inner access to the royal palace, could not keep silent.

The writer of Kings, peering out from deep within the Babylonian exile nearly two hundred years later, had a great deal to say about the root cause of Israel's demise: it was because "the sons of Israel had sinned against the LORD their God" and turned aside after foreign gods (2 Kgs 17:7-41). While Isaiah certainly would have agreed with this overall assessment, his own understanding of the problem was not that Israel chased after foreign gods *per se*, but that such apostasy inevitably led to a deplorable lack of justice and righteousness throughout the land, weakening the moral fiber of the nation and hence its resolve to withstand foreign threats (eg. Isa 5:7; 9:8-21). Because Isaiah's point of view was from within, it was current, practical and anything but simplistic. Now that the northern kingdom was gone and Assyria was still on the march, Isaiah understood all too well that this threat was just as real for Judah as it had been for Israel

Sargon II succeeded his father Shalmaneser in 722 B.C., just as Samaria was being annexed to the Assyrian empire. Two years later he faced an initial setback on the battlefield east of the Tigris River, prompting what was left of the native populations of the Levant to revolt against Assyrian rule. Sargon's own annals indicate that Judah also joined the fray.[28] All came to naught as the Assyrian king quickly put down the revolt in a battle at Raphia, a city of the southern coastal plain between Gaza and the River of Egypt (*Wadi el-Arish* in the Sinai). Realizing that his entire western flank (and access to Egypt) was no longer in friendly hands, Ahaz wisely capitulated before the fight reached Jerusalem. Over the next decade Sargon worked to mop up the entire Philistine coastal plain. In Judah, meanwhile, Ahaz died and was succeeded by his son Hezekiah who inherited a kingdom nearly bereft of hope (2 Chron 28:27—29:2).

Hezekiah was just the king Judah needed. Full of energy and ambition and loyal to the LORD God and temple priesthood in Jerusalem, Hezekiah sought to revive the national strength of Judah, albeit tempered somewhat by the pragmatic counsel of Isaiah. Quite early in his reign, Hezekiah re-instituted the Passover festival, a celebration that had not been properly observed in Jerusalem since the days of David and Solomon (2 Chron 29:3—30:27). Hezekiah hoped to restore Judean influence "from Dan to Beer-sheva" (2 Chron 30:5), but realistically was only able to bring the remnants of Samaria (Ephraim and Manasseh) into the Judean fold (2 Chron 31:1-2). His efforts were wisely focused on religious festivals and cult centers, matters that Sargon let slide so long as Judah's payments of tribute were not affected.

Sargon, in any case, was busy elsewhere, campaigning across Assyria's vast frontier. He reached the Philistine coast again in both 713 and 712 B.C., squelching revolts by the kings of Ashdod that had been egged on by Egypt's pharaoh Shabako. Edom, Moab and Judah all had a hand in Ashdod's insurrection, and Isaiah strongly and publicly urged Hezekiah to leave well enough alone. This time Isaiah's actions spoke louder than his words. For three years the prophet walked the streets of Jerusalem without shoes or sackcloth, "naked and barefoot"—although probably with loincloth in place—as a graphic sign that Assyria would so lead Egypt into exile, clothed only in the shame of nakedness (Isa 20:1-6). Apparently Hezekiah needed both a strong sign and a continual reminding to not disturb the status quo, and so Isaiah, prominent resident of Jerusalem that he was, placed the future of his people above his own reputation and comfort. In the meantime, Sargon had his own way on the Philistine coastal plain, turning the region into the Assyrian province of Ashdod. Judah was now surrounded.

Sargon died on the battlefield in the mountains of eastern Anatolia in 705 B.C. and was succeeded by his son Sennacherib. Sensing (or maybe just hoping) that Assyria was headed into a period of instability, Hezekiah saw his chance. For the last seven years he had prudently and dutifully paid tribute to Sargon, but now no longer (2 Kgs 18:7). Revolt spread like wildfire from Babylon to the Levant. Hezekiah immediately moved to strengthen his kingdom: if Assyria stayed away, perhaps Judah could assume the role as the major player in the southern Levant, but even if Sennacherib returned (and Hezekiah knew that he must), he would be ready for the fight. And so the Judean king fortified a number of cities at strategic junctures or on observation points throughout the hill country of Judah and in the Shephelah, and outfitted them with provisions and armaments for war, pushing Judah's influence "as far as Gaza and its territory" (2 Kgs 18:8). Archaeological excavations at Lachish, Judah's second capital and a royal chariot city (cf. Micah 1:13a) overlooking the coastal plain to the southwest have uncovered evidence of impressive fortifications.[29]

But it was Jerusalem that received most of the attention. Hezekiah expanded the size of the walled-in area of the section of Jerusalem that had been David's city and encircled the broad hill lying immediately to its west with a massive wall. It was here that refugees from Israel and others looking for protection and better economic opportunities had settled over the course of the last several de-

JERUSALEM, 701 B.C.

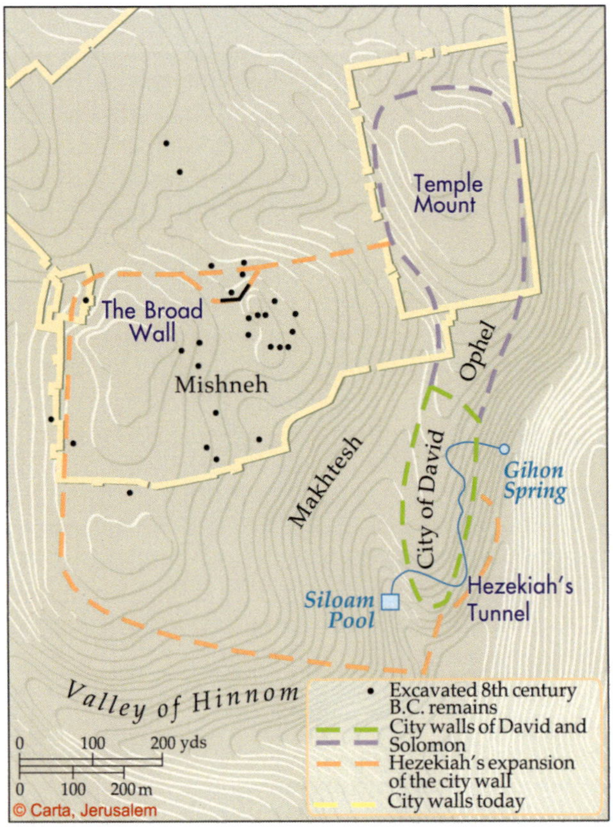

cades. He also improved the city's water supply by having gangs of workmen hew a 1750-foot long conduit through solid rock (the so-called "Hezekiah's Tunnel") to channel the water of the Gihon spring to a large pool within the city walls (2 Kgs 20:20; 2 Chron 32:30). South of Jerusalem, on a prominent rise exactly half-way to Bethlehem (at modern Ramat Rachel), Hezekiah built for himself a magnificent royal palace in the style of the now-destroyed palaces of the northern kingdom of Israel. After the fighting was over, Isaiah looked back and described Hezekiah's war preparations this way (with explanatory comments added):

In that day you depended on the weapons of the Forest House
[the armory];
You saw that there were many breaches in [the wall of] the city of David
[so you repaired them];
You collected the waters of the lower pool
[to withstand a prolonged siege];
You counted the houses of Jerusalem
[in order to expropriate their land]
and tore them down
[since they lay in the way]
to fortify the wall;
And you made a reservoir between the two walls for the waters of the old pool.
But—you didn't depend on the One who made it,
nor did you take into consideration the One who planned all this long ago.

(Isa 22:8b–11)

Isaiah was all in favor of a strong kingdom and a healthy national economy, and was probably impressed with Hezekiah's skills in administration and governance, as far as they went. But having a paid-up insurance policy, Isaiah cautioned his king, was a poor use of resources if it lulled its owner (and beneficiaries!) into the complacency of self-sufficiency.

Isaiah and Hezekiah were colleagues, their missions in life intertwined though they didn't always see eye-to-eye. As an example, Isaiah provided medical treatment when Hezekiah suffered a life-threatening illness (2 Kgs 20:1–7; Isa 38:1–22), then promptly called his king to account when he snuggled too closely with one of his well-wishers, Merodach-baladan, king of Babylon—Judah *would* go into exile, but to Babylon, not Assyria (2 Kgs 20:16–19; Isa 39:5–8). Hezekiah's response was tragic to the core: "The word of the LORD is good," he told the prophet, feigning acceptance of Isaiah's words, while all the while thinking "So what? At least there will be peace in *my* days." But Isaiah's eyesight was crystal-clear (cf. Isa 6:8-10) and saw right through his transparent king: It was bad enough that the moral failing of the people Judah was taking its toll on the spirit of the nation, but now the king, too? The very best that the house of David had to offer was falling short at the exact moment of its biggest crisis. Isaiah now knew that his most important message to Judah must be not only that God would intervene on Israel's behalf (for judgment or deliverance) in times of intense national stress, but that one day he would step into history in a personal and redemptive way far greater than could be done through a normal king of Judah (Isa 41:8–20; 42:1–9; 49:1–7; 50:4–11; 52:13–53:12; 61:1–9).

In the meantime there was a battle to fight. Sennacherib's goal was to force Judah back into the Assyrian fold. According to Assyrian annals, his army drove to the Philistine Coastal Plain, then plunged into Judah from the west, through the valleys of the Shephelah.[30] The siege of Lachish was the decisive battle, and when Sennacherib eventually returned to Nineveh he commissioned his artisans to portray the full assault and violent end to Lachish in all its brilliant and gory detail in high relief on one of the most prominent walls of his royal palace. When the fate of Lachish was certain, Sennacherib sent his emissary, the Rabshakeh,[31] to Jerusalem to demand Hezekiah's surrender (2 Kgs 18:17–37; Isa 36:1–22). In Sennacherib's own words, Hezekiah was now trapped "like a bird in a cage."[32] Realizing that his enormous efforts to prepare Judah for the assault were no match for the Assyrian onslaught, Hezekiah finally turned to the LORD for help—something Isaiah had been counseling all along (2 Kgs 19:1–34; Isa 37:1–35). It was only then that Sennacherib broke off the siege of Jerusalem and returned home, eventually to be murdered back in Nineveh though not until Hezekiah himself had died (2 Kgs 19:8–9, 35–37; Isa 37:8, 36–38; cf. Mic 1:10–16). The kingdom of Judah was devastated; only Jerusalem survived—and that, just barely.

Sennacherib's attack on Jerusalem is one of very few events described in the Old Testament three times (2 Kings 18–19, 2 Chronicles 32 and Isaiah 36–37). Clearly this greatest moment of crisis was a pivotal point in the ebb and flow of the nation of Judah. It was not the Judeans' finest hour—but it was God's, and His prophet, Isaiah, had the vision to lift his eyes to the larger picture. Like his kings Isaiah, too, was a realist, but of a very different kind: One who had come to terms with the failings of the human potential for good and stare full-face into the shortcomings of his people. But he was also a visionary, for whom the normal rules of political science didn't apply. Rather, the prophet declared that the entire event had been orchestrated by God long before in order to show his divine power over the affairs of men (Isa 37:26–35). If Jerusalem survived—and both it and a remnant of its people surely would—it was because God had ordained such from the beginning of time. The One who herds the starry host as if it were a flock of sheep (Isa 40:26) would surely protect his own people. For the prophet, living in deeply troubled times, this was comfort enough (Isa 40:1–2, 21–31). And so Isaiah looked to the future.

JOSIAH

The biblical writers saw periods of renewal in ancient Israel as a divine work, a time when God favored the efforts of a righteous and capable king, and both people and nation thrived. Behind such an assessment we can see their approval of a situation in which influential forces within priestly and prophetic circles became aligned with the throne (though who might have actually called the shots in any situation is a matter of debate). The reign of Josiah is the textbook example of such things coming together, made even more significant in the light of cataclysmic events on the world stage in which Judah was necessarily—though not always willingly—involved.

The Assyrian attack of 701 B.C. had left the people of Judah staggering, their land devastated and local economy in ruins. One of the greatest challenges facing Hezekiah and his successor, Manasseh, was how to restore the hope and fortunes of Judah without arousing the ire of their new overlord, which needed a pacified Levant as it made its final imperialistic drive into Egypt. Scholars have labeled the first half of the seventh century B.C. a time of *Pax Assyriaca,*[33] when the "peace of Assyria" governed the political, social and economic priorities of the lands bordering the eastern seaboard of the Mediterranean. Eventually Jerusalem's religious hierarchy would interpret the survival of Judah as proof that God would never let Jerusalem, his chosen city, fall (cf. Jer 7:4). In the meantime, we can easily assume that the competent and freedom-loving Hezekiah spent his last years greatly frustrated by what could have been.

Hezekiah died in 686 B.C.; the reign of his son Manasseh (who died in 642 B.C.) was the longest tenure of any king of the Divided Monarchy. It must have provided a measure of relief for war-weary Judah. Manasseh was, on the whole, an accommodator when it came to foreign relations, calculating that Judah's best chance for revival lay in its ability to appease the priorities of those who shared its orbit (cf. 2 Kgs 21:5; 23:11–13; Jer 7:17–18; 19:13; Zeph 1:8). The priestly and prophetic circles of Jerusalem were understandably angered (2 Kgs 21:12–13). Nevertheless, it seems as though Manasseh's policies, combined with the stability of his long reign, allowed Judah to begin to regain its economic footing.

Hezekiah's vision for a renewed Judah was hampered by the grip of the Assyrian vice, while Manasseh's ran afoul of powerful circles in Jerusalem. For most of the seventh century B.C., the pieces just didn't come together right. Manasseh's son and successor Amon reigned for only two years (642–640 B.C.) before being assassinated by his own servants, that is, persons who held official positions within the government (2 Kgs 21:19–23; cf. 2 Kgs 14:19). Clearly the royal bureaucracy was not happy with the direction that Amon was taking Judah, although not enough information is available to determine the source of their discontent. In any case, the "people of the land," a group of influential landed aristocrats who, though not of the royal blood line, had a history of exercising their will in affairs of state, promptly killed the assassins and placed Amon's eight-year old son Josiah on the throne (2 Kgs 21:24–26; cf. 2 Kgs 11:19–20; 14:21). So we should understand that Josiah began his reign with the support of a very significant element of Judean society (cf. 2 Chron 35:24–25), but also that he was chosen as king because he was young enough to be shaped by their will. *What* that will might have been can only be implied from the kind of king that Josiah turned out to be.

Assyria reached the zenith of their empire when Ashurbanipal sacked Thebes, the hoary religious and cultural center of Egypt, in 663 B.C., then went into an immediate and unrecoverable decline (they would cease to exist as an empire in just four short decades). Sensing the future of international affairs and seizing the moment of Amon's demise, the forces of conservative, religious nationalism in Judah took action to "train up [Josiah] in the way he should go" with the intent that when he came of age, "he would not depart from [their agenda]" (cf. Prov 22:6).

The writers of the books of Kings and Chronicles were wholly taken by the religious aspects of Josiah's reign, and by all indications his was the most thoroughgoing of the revivals in ancient Judah. The Chronicler gives the chronology: in Josiah's eighth year "while he was still a youth, he began to seek the God of his father David"; in his twelfth year "he began to purge Judah and Jerusalem of the high places" and other aspects of foreign and indigenous cults; and in his eighteenth year he gave instruction "to repair the house of the LORD his God" and "celebrate the Passover to the LORD in Jerusalem" (2 Chron 34:3, 8; 35:1). These dates should not necessarily be taken as an exact sequence of individual events but

THE SOUTHERN LEVANT DURING THE REIGN OF MANASSEH

THE KINGDOM OF JUDAH IN THE DAYS OF JOSIAH

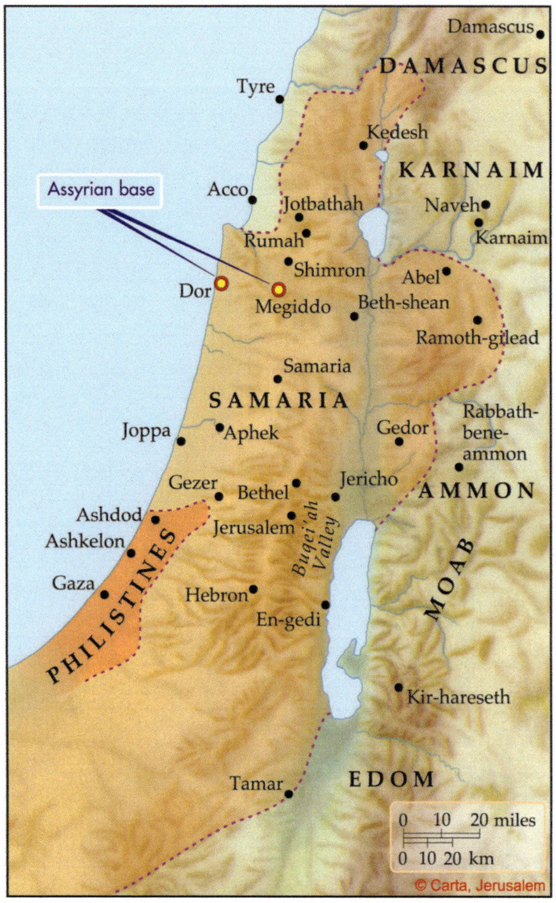

rather as well-positioned summary statements of a lifetime of royal effort to return Judah to the glory days of David and Solomon. The Chronicler's outline gives logical coherence to the events, but also makes historical-geographical (and common) sense. Indeed, each of these dates (years eight, twelve and eighteen of Josiah's reign) correspond to other actions or events that impacted the life of the young king and offered him both the opportunity and encouragement to pursue a path of greatness.

Josiah's first formative years, before his eighth year on the throne, were spent under the guidance of "the people of the land," those influential voices of conservatism that had brought him to power. He responded well to their tutelage. His son Jehoahaz (also called Shallum; 1 Chron 3:15; Jer 22:11) was born in Josiah's fateful eighth year, when the king was sixteen (cf. 2 Kgs 22:1). The mother of Jehoahaz, Hamutal, Josiah's favorite wife, was from Libnah, a Levitical priestly city in the southwestern Shephelah (2 Kgs 23:31; cf. Josh 21:13; 1 Chron 6:57). The Levitical cities were centers of religious and political conservatism in Judah and probably served as regional focal points for the work of the "people of the land." It is reasonable to think, then, that Josiah had been shaped by the political and religious priorities of his father-in-law's family from Libnah. As he came of age and faced the reality of not only governing a kingdom but raising a family, Josiah chose to embrace what he had been taught to hold dear from childhood and "began [personally] to seek the God of his father David" (2 Chron 34:3). It was a fortuitous choice.

The tenor of Josiah's reign was put into force in the years that followed, and is summarized in a long list of reforms recorded by the writers of Kings and Chronicles that were instituted by the king between his twelfth and eighteenth years on the throne (2 Kgs 23:4–20; 2 Chron 34:3–7, 33). These reforms presuppose a resurgent nationalism that aimed to restore the political and religious fervor of the kingdom of David. They reached their climax in year eighteen (622 B.C.), when the Jerusalem temple was refurbished, the covenant with the LORD the God of Israel was renewed, and Passover, Israel's great freedom festival, was celebrated.

Josiah's twelfth year on the throne, 628 B.C., coincided with the death of Ashurbanipal, the last great king of the Assyrian empire. For the Judean king this was an open invitation to reclaim territory that not only had been converted into Assyrian provinces during the days of Jotham, Ahaz and Hezekiah one hundred years before, but to bring back into the Jerusalem fold the heartland of the Northern Kingdom of Israel that had stood in rebellion against the House of David for two long centuries prior. As a political leader, Josiah's destiny was clear.

But other factors also came into play during these critical years. The prophet Jeremiah began his ministry in 627 B.C., in the thirteenth year of Josiah's reign (Jer 1:2; 25:3). The prophetic ministry of Zephaniah, perhaps a man of the royal house (cf. Zeph 1:1), also coincided with Josiah's rule. Both prophets spoke forcefully of the dire straits into which the people of Judah and Jerusalem had fallen. Though their loudest message was one of impending judgment (Jer 3:1–5; Zeph 1:7–18; 3:6), it was a tirade consistent with Josiah's call for reform (cf. Jer 3:20–4:1; Zeph 3:8–11). The irony is that Judah saw its greatest potential for social, moral and religious revival only on the eve of its final destruction. Like Assyria, Judah's flame burned brightest just before it went out. Josiah stood in as the last great hope.

To protect his land and expand its limited economy, Josiah pushed outward. Archaeological evidence suggests that he rebuilt or strengthened fortresses at Kadesh-barnea on the border between the Negev and Sinai (*Ain el-Qudeirat*)[34] and Arad, facing Edom. A small temple had stood within the walls of the Arad fortress since the days of Solomon, and Josiah, it seems, destroyed or dismantled it in the process of rebuilding the fort, part of his drive to centralize worship in Jerusalem.[35] Three small fortresses in the Buqei'ah, a small valley in the Judean Wilderness above the northwestern corner of the Dead Sea (*Kh. Abu Tabaq, Kh. es-Samrah* and *Kh. el-Maqari*, possibly the Middin, Secacah and Nibsham of Josh 15:61–62, respectively), might also be attributed to Josiah.[36] In addition to their military value guarding the approaches to Jerusalem from the east, these fortresses, with nearby dams and catchment basins for runoff rainfall, seem to have been an attempt to wrest agricultural productivity from an otherwise stark and arid landscape.

But Judah's main points of access lay to the west, and it is here that the king had the strongest incentive and opportunity to make a stand. Josiah's mother, Jedidah, was from Bozkath (2 Kgs 22:1), a village far out in the southwestern Shephelah (Josh 15:37–41) and his wife Hamutal came from Libnah, a prominent city in the vicinity (2 Kgs 23:31; cf. Josh 15:42). These family ties drew Josiah's interests to the far side of the Shephelah, within striking distance of the coast and the scene of so much international threat in the past. While the practical extent of Josiah's interests out on the coast remains unclear, the large L-shaped fortress of Mezad Hashavyahu midway between Jaffa and Ashdod indicates that Josiah did maintain control over at least part of the plain.[37] What ties this site to Judah specifically is the discovery of an ostracon, written in good biblical Hebrew and containing a Yahwistic personal name, *Hashavyahu*. The subject matter of the text shows that Judeans were also able to settle and farm the region and that the standards of justice advocated in the ancient Mosaic law still formed the basis for complaint and redress.

Of course Josiah also looked north. The Chronicler notes that Josiah's efforts reached "even as far as Naphtali" (2 Chron 34:6), bringing the Sea of Galilee (the Kinneret) and Upper Galilee into the Judean fold and pushing the northern limits of his control toward Dan. Archaeological evidence at Megiddo shows that a fortress was erected on top of Assyrian remains in the late seventh century B.C.[38] Indeed, enough clues exist for us to assume that Josiah's kingdom reached to most, if not all, of the regions embraced by the old Solomonic phrase "from Dan to Beer-sheba" (cf. 1 Kgs 4:25). Politically it was Judah's last great hurrah, one in which Josiah was able to find enough jockey-room among the remnants of the local kingdoms of the southern Levant to fill the vacuum left by the collapse of Assyria.

Politics aside, for Bible readers the more visible aspects of the revival of Josiah's kingdom were those that impacted its religion. Foremost among these were his efforts to purge Jerusalem and Judah of the high places and ritual objects associated with deities other than the LORD (2 Kgs 23:4–5, 11–13; cf. 1 Kgs 11:7–8). Josiah also rooted out the cults of Baal and Asherah, the persistent, indigenous deities of the land who had taken up residence in Jerusalem and even in the temple (2 Kgs 23:4–10, 14; 2 Chron 34:3–4). This part of the purge was bloody, and many of the priests attached to cultic sites in Samaria were killed, "slaughtered on the altars" according to the writer of Kings in a fate most fitting their deeds (2 Kgs 23:20). The force of Josiah's purge, however, was directed at those who were spiritually closest to home, the priests of the LORD God who served local shrines throughout the towns and villages of Judah and "burned incense from Geba to Beer-sheba" (2 Kgs 23:8). Their worship centers were destroyed and, in a move aimed at centralizing worship, Josiah bade them come to Jerusalem, the only remaining legitimate center of worship for the LORD. The temple priests who were already residing in Jerusalem, with their own established interests to protect, weren't keen on the idea and most of the local priests preferred to stay back home (2 Kgs 23:8–9). In any case, the result was that these men, each of whom was probably the most influential person in their respective home towns, were alienated from the larger flow of events that were redefining the kingdom. It was the downside of Josiah's reform.

A fortuitous find provided the mechanism for legitimizing and perpetuating this reform. During repair work on the Jerusalem temple, the high priest Hilkiah reported that he had found "the book of the law" somewhere within the confines of the building (2 Kgs 22:8). The scholarly consensus, suggested by no less a man of learning than Jerome, holds that the document that was found was some form of the book of Deuteronomy, a book that speaks precisely to the spiritual, political and lifestyle concerns of Judah in the closing days of its kingdom. Indeed, the "deuteronomists" (as the conservative forces that supported and guided Josiah on the throne have been called), were finally able to legitimize the ancient traditions of the divine Yahwistic covenant that had remained alive in Israel and Judah all along. More importantly, this book of the law ensured that the ideals of Josiah's reform would remain alive even if the nation slid into apostasy and exile.

But everything came to a screeching halt in 609 B.C., when Josiah was thirty-nine years old and at the height of his reign. In what would be a failed attempt to stop the surging Babylonians, heirs to the Assyrian Empire in the Levant, the Egyptians under Necho II marched straight up the coast, through land that was part of Josiah's revived kingdom. Josiah faced Necho at Megiddo, where he met an untimely death (2 Kgs 23:29–30; 2 Chron 35:20–24). The episode is tragic beyond all measure, and leaves many questions unanswered. Why did Josiah pick a fight with the Egyptians? Did he hope to catch Egypt unprepared and conquer Egypt outright? And why make the challenge at Megiddo rather than at Lachish, Gezer or Aphek, all points the Egyptian army would have had to pass on the way and all closer to Judah and hence more easily defended by Josiah? Did Josiah actually think that his small kingdom could succeed against the great empires of the day, or was he so overcome with zeal that his judgment was clouded? In fact, more likely it was Necho who initiated the rendezvous, calling Josiah to Megiddo, the site of a centuries-old Egyptian base in Canaan, to secure an oath of loyalty, and Josiah seized the opportunity to push Judah's expansion to its logical conclusion.

Josiah was badly wounded in battle, shot through by an Egyptian arrow. The rip through his body must have been excruciating, and all the more so on the long, torturous journey back to Jerusalem, the stricken king wrapped in what would become his death-shroud and huddled on the floor of his chariot, bouncing along from rut to rock, in and out of wadis, with each jolt searing his nerves and shocking his brain. It was a long time to think, and Josiah must have replayed the events of his entire life over and over in his mind: "Why this? Why now?" Like Abel, righteous, just and so full of unrealized promise, Josiah was cut down in his prime (cf. Gen 4:1–8). Eventually blood poisoning would have set in and, like countless soldiers before and since who survived an initial battle wound (cf. 1 Sam 31:3–4; 1 Kgs 22:34–35), Josiah succumbed in delirium and pain.

The nation's agony was no less acute:

> All Judah and Jerusalem mourned for Josiah. Then Jeremiah chanted a lament for the king. All the male and female singers speak about Josiah in their lamentations to this day. (2 Chron 35:24b–25)

The swell tide of reform dropped overnight, leaving the residue from the bottom to define the future of the kingdom. Josiah's youngest son, Jehoahaz, was also made king by "the people of the land," but he cared little for their conservative ways or the religious aspects of the reforms of his father ("he did evil in the sight of the LORD according to all that his fathers had done"; 2 Kgs 23:32). Within three months the Egyptians deposed Jehoahaz and placed his brother Eliakim (Jehoiakim) on the throne, effectively reducing Judah to a vassal state once again (2 Kgs 23:34–37). This began a chain of events that led to the destruction of Jerusalem and the temple, and the exile of Judah to Babylon twenty-three years later (2 Kgs 24:1–25:21). Caught between Assyria, Egypt and Babylon, Judean independence had lasted scarcely two decades. Josiah had fostered an environment whereby prophets such as Jeremiah and Zephaniah could gain a hearing that even his successors couldn't silence (e.g., Jer 26:7–24). We can only suppose what could have happened if the effort, like the life of the king, had not been cut short in its prime.

Shaphan reading the book of the law before King Josiah (2 Kgs 22:8–10), *19th century engraving* (Carta, Jerusalem).

JOHN THE BAPTIST

The early part of the first century A.D. was a fairly prosperous time for the Jewish residents of Judea and Galilee, all things considered, and a significant percentage of the population was learning to work within the Romanized political and economic systems that had enveloped their land. Still, many were looking for "the Elijah that was to come" (cf. Mal 4:5–6), though it was difficult to agree on exactly what his appearance would entail in real terms. When John the Baptist came "preaching in the wilderness of Judea, crying out: "Repent, for the Kingdom of Heaven is at hand!" (Mt 3:1), dressed like the Elijah of old and playing the already ancient prophetic role to the hilt, he drew decidedly mixed reactions. It wasn't exactly a bolt out of the prophetic blue—others also were claiming prophetic (or even messianic) roles (cf. Acts 5:33–39)—but John certainly cast a jarring counter-culture pose and in the end even gained the attention of Herod Antipas, the governing tetrarch. But for the writers of the Gospels John the Baptist was the real thing, the long-awaited flesh and blood arc spanning the chasm of time and binding the God-spoken Testament of Moses with the New Testament of the long-awaited Anointed One, Jesus the Messiah (Lk 16:16).

A role as special as this required a special kind of birth. Both of John's parents, Zechariah and Elizabeth, were of priestly descent (Lk 1:5), a two-fold honor in the day. Luke describes them as "righteous in the sight of God and walking blamelessly in all the commandments and requirements of the LORD" (Lk 1:6); that is, devout folk living responsible lives with all proper public and private expressions of first-century Judaism in place. Zechariah was an active priest, one, it seems, for whom the priesthood was a sincere calling, unencumbered by the aristocratic tendencies that seemed to seize too many of his colleagues up in Jerusalem during the last years of the reign of Herod the Great. He and Elizabeth were well along in years but childless, and carried together the public stigma that God had withheld his blessing in spite of their lifetime of faithful service to him (cf. Lk 1:25).

MARY'S VISIT TO ELIZABETH

Zechariah belonged to the priestly division of Abijah, one of twenty-four groupings of priests who served in the Jerusalem temple (Lk 1:5; cf. 1 Chron 24:1–19). Each individual from each of the priestly divisions had the opportunity to offer personally the daily incense offering in the temple, but because of the large number of priests this honor came only a very few times—perhaps only once—in a lifetime. After the incense was burned, the day's officiating priest customarily lingered alone before the altar—just outside the door of the Holy of Holies—to bring his private petitions to God.[39] In what was likely Zechariah's last time to stand in this holy place, the chief angel Gabriel suddenly appeared and promised that not only would Elizabeth become pregnant, their much-awaited child would be a most special son, born in the ascetic, separatist tradition of the biblical Nazirites (Lk 1:8–15, 19; cf. Num 6:1–21; Judg 13:4–5, 14). Moreover, he would enter the world in the spirit and power of Elijah "to turn the hearts of the fathers back to the children and the disobedient to the attitude of the righteous, so as to make ready a people prepared for the LORD" (Lk 1:17; cf. Mal 4:6), indeed, be the forerunner of someone even greater than he.

Everything happened exactly as Gabriel said. Six months into her pregnancy Elizabeth had a special visitor: Mary, a near relative, who had also received an angelic visit and was in the beginning stages of her own divine pregnancy. The expectant mothers knew that something quite extraordinary was happening, and the two formed a special bond (Lk 1:26–56). So would their sons.

Nothing is known of John's formative years except that he grew in body, mind and Spirit, like Samson and Samuel before and Jesus to follow (Lk 1:80; cf. Judg 13:24–25; 1 Sam 3:19; Lk 2:40). Luke identified John's hometown as only a village in the hill country of Judea (Lk 1:39, 65), though church tradition has localized the site as Encharim, modern En Kerem in the far western suburbs of Jerusalem. The village is nestled in a wonderfully picturesque valley, far enough from Jerusalem to be surrounded by expanses of "open countryside" (so "deserts" or "empty places" should be rendered in Luke 1:80) in which a young John must have often hiked and explored. It was an optimistic landscape, mirroring the unbounded expectations that Zechariah had set for his one and only son (Lk 1:67–79).

Were it not for the unusual circumstances of his birth, John would certainly have followed in his father's footsteps as the local village priest, serving dutifully in the Jerusalem temple as his turn came due, together with the next generation of priests of the division of Abijah. It is likely that he did so at first, before what Luke termed "the day of his public appearance to Israel" (Lk 1:80). Service in Jerusalem would have given John ample opportunity to see first-hand the excesses, insincerity and corruption that had come to infect too much of the Herodian-style temple leadership in his day. Certainly a righteous anger that was as pointed as John's must have been honed on the anvil of personal experience.

Sometime in A.D. 28 or 29 (cf. Lk 3:1–3), when John was a

THE MINISTRY OF JOHN THE BAPTIST

little over 30 years old, he climbed over the Mount of Olives and withdrew deep into the wilderness of Judea, to the arid wasteland above the northern end of the Dead Sea. Traditionally, such wilderness areas were places of death, purification and rebirth (cf. Deut 32:10–12; Jer 2:6–7; Ezek 47:1–12; Hos 2:3–4, 14–20, etc.), and so the region formed an appropriate backdrop for the ascetic prophet. Something altruistic seems to have been involved, and the overall impression given by the writers of the Gospels depicts a man who was genuinely moved by the power-sanctioned injustices of his day, sacrificing his own reputation and career as a young priest to call the entire system into account. Priests tended to be members of The Establishment while Old Testament-style prophets usually stood counter-culture (beneath their wrathful front was a broken heart), and John's divine call as the latter drove him from the comforts of home to a life of alienation in a place wild and alone. It was a willful move throughout, and this as much as anything likely prompted his former colleagues from Jerusalem to make the trek into the harsh wilderness to see what the fuss was all about. Those who made it down got an earful. It's not easy to be called a snake by one's (former) colleague (Mt 3:7–10; Lk 3:7–9).

With mixed doses of venom and sarcasm, John didn't leave a lot of room for self-justification or philosophical discussions. What is surprising is not that Pharisees and Sadducees came to John in order to submit to his baptism (Mt 3:7), but that he dismissed them out of hand, likely sensing insincerity or mixed motives. But some people—perhaps many—did respond favorably. Luke calls them "the multitude" (Lk 3:7, 10; cf. Mt 3:5; Mk 1:5), the common folk who constantly fill the background of the Gospel story. Of those who were particularly moved (or who had little to go back to), some remained and became disciples; Elijah had had a school of prophets in the same area (2 Kgs 2:15). Most, however, certainly returned home to their families and jobs, changed for the better for the effort of seizing the grip that God had placed on their lives. One of these was Andrew, brother of Simon Peter (Jn 1:40); both would one day become disciples of Jesus.

John's intended audience also included tax collectors and soldiers—collaborators and Gentiles who represented and enforced the everyday face of Rome (Lk 3:12, 14). His message to them was not that they should quit their jobs but that they should treat others fairly, righteously and honorably in the normal course of their duties (Lk 3:12–14). He demanded no more or no less of everyone else (Lk 3:10–11). John didn't advocate political change; he only demanded that the political system—be it Rome or Jerusalem-based—govern benevolently (this was bound to anger both zealots and friends of Caesar). It was the Kingdom of Heaven that was coming (Mt 3:1), and for John, personally-changed lives that could influence society for good was the key to getting ready for it.

Those who responded by confessing their sins were baptized (Mt 3:5–6; Mk 1:4–5; Lk 3:3). While ritual acts of washing were common in Judaism in the first century A.D., there must have been something particularly striking about John's immersion, "a baptism of repentance for the remission of sins," that gave him the nickname "the Baptist" (or, "the Baptizer;" Mt 3:1; Mk 1:4–5). John the Baptist made no mention of any of the priestly ceremonial rites that characterized either normative Judaism or the teachings of the nearby Qumran community, including the need to repeatedly purify one's body through ritual washings. Instead, he made a direct connection between right living and a one-time immersion that signaled that the individual had adopted (or was in the process of adopting) a lifestyle characterized by acts of justice and righteousness, and had (or was) sincerely repenting of his sins. It was a bold, visible and decisive way of signaling the need for both Jews and Gentiles (everyone from Sadducees to Roman soldiers) to start over, as it were, from scratch ("don't call yourselves children of Abraham…"; Mt 3:8). In essence, John's baptism undercut an important cornerstone of Jerusalem's temple apparatus (and of Qumran) in favor of direct access to God. It was, in the words of Mark, "the beginning of the gospel (lit., 'good news') of Jesus Christ" (Mt 1:1; cf. Acts 1:22; 10:37).

John didn't exactly fit any of his contemporary modes—neither the Pharisees or Sadducees, not the residents of Qumran or the social or political critics of his day, not even the messianic hopefuls who, with the exception of Jesus, all looked for the overthrow of Rome. His message was religious, but with clear social and political implications. These implications were welcomed by the masses, although they seem to have been aimed particularly at people who held enough institutionalized power to effect real change. In spite of his clear ties to the mainstream Judaism of his day, perhaps the best way to characterize John is by the words of all four Evangelists (who quoted the Greek Septuagint text of Isaiah 40:3): he was "a Voice Crying in the Wilderness" (cf. Mt 3:3; Mk 1:3; Lk 3:4 and Jn 1:23).

John's prophetic ministry took him up and down the Jordan Valley, where he encountered many people on both sides of the river (Mt 3:1; Jn 1:28; 3:23; 10:40).[40] It was a region that had been frequented by Elijah (1 Kgs 17:1–7; 2 Kgs 2:1–14); the two even ate off the land and dressed in a similar fashion (Mt 3:4; 11:18; Mk 1:6; cf. 1 Kgs 17:6; Zech 13:4; Mal 4:5–6). It was at Bethany

John the Baptist was an itinerant prophet, moving up and down the Jordan River and to places such as Aenon near Salim (Jn 3:23), wherever there was water to baptize and interest in what he had to say. It is impossible to pinpoint any spot exactly, although church tradition certainly has tried. Quiet reflection at the edge of the Jordan River is sufficient to ponder his message.

beyond the Jordan that John met up with Jesus, his most significant candidate for baptism (Mt 3:13–17; Mk 1:9–11; Lk 3:21–22; Jn 1:19–34). This was the beginning of Jesus' public ministry, and the climax of John's. Jesus, who apparently had been watching John's activities with keen interest from afar, came to the prophet from his home in Nazareth of Galilee. John seems to have known who Jesus was as well, although the realization that this was the one for whom he had been preparing the way now struck John with full force (Jn 1:29–34). He was at first put off by Jesus' request to be baptized, then relented "to fulfill all righteousness" (Mt 3:14–15; cf. Jn 1:26–27, 30).

From this point on John fades from the scene of the Gospel story. He would have approved: "[Jesus] must increase," the Baptist later told his disciples, "and I must decrease" (Jn 3:30). Understandably, some of them had trouble with the idea and were a little jealous of Jesus' success which appeared to detract from the work of their own master (Jn 3:26). John could have solved the problem by simply disbanding his own ministry in favor of that of Jesus, since his specific calling had been to prepare the way for Jesus' appearance in the first place. But he continued to preach and baptize to all who still would come, and Jesus even seems to have endorsed his ministry when he headed back into Galilee so as not to visibly override John's work (Jn 4:1–3).

John's prophetic ministry, in any case, could not have lasted much longer. Altogether it covered no more than a year (or two at the most) from start to finish. His work was cut short when he was arrested and put in prison—familiar ground for prophets, to be sure—ostensibly because of personal criticism of the conduct of the tetrarch, Herod Antipas (Mt 14:3–12; Mk 6:14–29; Lk 9:7–9). John publicly called Antipas to account for divorcing his wife to marry Herodias, the wife of his half-brother, Philip. John's point could have been that Antipas' divorce was foolish politically, since the tetrarch's divorced wife was a powerful Nabatean queen whose territory bordered that of the tetrarch, but ramifications on the nation-state level didn't concern the prophet. For the Gospel writers, Antipas was irked that John had held him to the same moral standards of everyone else. According to Josephus, Antipas feared that John the Baptist was growing too powerful among the masses and might launch a rebellion (*Ant.* xviii.118). Mixed motives are appropriate in regard to this multi-faceted prophet. John was beheaded at Machaerus (*Ant.* xviii.119), a Herodian palace-prison-fortress in Perea, near the Nabatean border, at a bawdy birthday party for Antipas.

John's disciples were granted the right to their leader's decapitated body and buried what was left of his remains with all the dignity they could muster in a location not mentioned by either the Gospel writers or Josephus. Despondent, they informed Jesus of the affair (Mt 14:12). To whom else could they go?

When John was still in prison, facing the cold stone walls and a diet that probably made him *wish* he had locusts and wild honey—not knowing if he would be executed although the grisly thought must have crossed his mind—he questioned whether or not this Jesus whom he had baptized really was the one who would vindicate the bold turn that his life had taken. Was it all worth it? Was Jesus going to pick up the pieces? Or would the momentum that was building for the Kingdom of Heaven stall out like it had when other messiah figures met an untimely death (cf. *Ant.* xiv.158–160; Acts 5:33–39; 21:38)? John sent some of his disciples to Jesus to ask if in fact he was the expected one. Jesus' reply was the reply of the obvious: the blind see, the lame walk, the lepers are cleansed, the deaf hear, the dead are raised up and the downtrodden are hearing the Good News (Mt 11:2–6; Lk 7:18–23). The coming Kingdom was in good hands. Then Jesus added, "Blessed is the one who doesn't stumble over me." This last comment wasn't for John's benefit, but the prophet's disciples. What would *they* do if their master was gone?

And now he was, and John's disciples had to make a choice. Some, such as the disciple Andrew of Bethsaida, brother of Simon Peter, attached themselves to Jesus' growing band (Jn 1:35–42). Others probably scattered or went back home, as Jesus' own disciples (including Andrew) would do soon after the crucifixion (cf. Mt 26:56; Jn 21:1–3). But some remained loyal to John; baptized by him, they followed and promoted his teachings and manner of baptism, fasting and prayer (cf. Mk 2:18; Lk 11:1). John's movement remained alive and gained ground even outside of the land of Israel, in Egypt and in Asia Minor. Twenty-five years later, in the mid-50's A.D., the Apostle Paul met a group of around twelve people in Ephesus who believed in Jesus, yet had only been baptized according to the baptism of John. Apparently they had learned of John (and perhaps even Jesus) through Apollos of Alexandria, who had since moved on to Corinth (Acts 18:24–25; 19:1–3; cf. 1 Cor 1:10–13). How Apollos learned about John in the first place is not known, but the cosmopolitan Jewish community in Alexandria did have ongoing contact with Jerusalem, and an eloquent man such as himself may well have been well connected to channels of learning and thought throughout the Jewish world.

For many of the Jews of Jerusalem and Judea, John the Baptist was a rather pointed reminder that a life worth living was a life characterized by deeds of righteousness. For the emerging Christian movement across the Roman world, John was a bridge to Jesus. But for Jesus, John was a prophet—yet more than a prophet:

> Truly, I say to you, among those born of women there has not arisen anyone greater than John the Baptist, yet he who is least in the Kingdom of Heaven is greater than he. (Mt 11:11)

It's quite an assessment for someone who made quite a scene during his lifetime. And it's also quite an honor, comparatively speaking, for those who followed.

JESUS

How do we begin to define Jesus? Common terms for greatness just don't work. More helpful are descriptive nouns that arise from aspects of the Gospel story: rabbinic scholar, skilled worker, friend, son, servant, deliverer, king; and while these are all certainly aspects of the whole, each by itself is too limiting. So too the biblical titles, some used by Jesus, some by others about him: Son of God (e.g., Mt 4:3; 8:29; 26:63); Son of Man (e.g., Mt 18:11; 25:31; 26:64); Rabbi (Jn 1:38); teacher (Mt 8:19); Lamb of God (Jn 1:36); Bread of Life (Jn 6:35); Light of the World (Jn 8:12); Good Shepherd (Jn 10:11); Word (Jn 1:1); even Lord (Jn 13:6). These are faces of a multi-faceted, highly complex and ultimately very successful individual; but even together they only begin to complete the whole. Perhaps the best is the one that most often defines Jesus today, the one that became his "last name": the Anointed One (Heb. *mashiach*/Messiah; Gk. *christos*/Christ; e.g., Mt 16:16; 27:22; Lk 2:11; 23:2; Jn 7:41–42; 11:27). "Messiah" was a title rooted in the fertile soil of Old Testament expectation, where it was usually attached to a priest (Lev 4:3, 5, 16; 6:22), a prophet (1 Chron 16:22; Ps 105:15) or a king (most notably Saul and David; 1 Sam 2:10; 16:6; 24:6; 26:9; 2 Sam 22:51; 23:1; Ps 2:2; 132:10) who had been christened (!) with oil and set apart for a special, above-the-norm task of leadership on behalf of the people of Israel.

The coming Messiah figured prominently in Jewish eschatological and apocalyptic literature of the period between the Testaments, giving witness about the time of the turn of the millennium to a heightened expectancy that God would deliver Israel from the cultural and political oppression of Hellenism and Rome (e.g., 1 Enoch 48:10; 52:4; Psalms of Solomon 17–18; 2 Esdras 12:31–33; Testament of Levi 18:2–14; and numerous texts and fragments from Qumran[41]). Indeed, the time was so ripe for deliverance that several self-appointed (self-anointed!) messiah-figures strove to the fore—usually from the religious and social matrix of Jerusalem or freedom-loving Galilee—gathered quick followings and then just as quickly foundered or were suppressed by the Roman authorities. Among these were Theudas, Judas the Galilean and his sons Jacob and Simon, Athronges, the Egyptian False Prophet and the Prophet in the Desert (Acts 5:36–37; 21:38; *Ant.* xvii.278–284; xx.97–104, 168–172, 185–188). Into this matrix (or was it a maelstrom?) came Jesus, who, according to the combined testimony of the writers of the Gospels and the Apostle Paul, was neither self-anointed nor anointed by someone with established temple or prophetic authority but from On High.

Having been specially chosen from before birth (from before *conception*; Lk 1:26–38), Jesus was born in Bethlehem of Judah (Mt 2:1–12; Lk 2:1–20), to Mary and Joseph of the line of David, righteous individuals who, from all appearances, were neither well-off nor dirt poor by situation. Joseph was a *tekton*, a skilled worker in local building materials[42] (Mt 13:55) from Nazareth, a small village off the main routes (and lines of easy employment) in Galilee. A reasonable case can be made that Joseph certainly, and likely even Jesus, as he "grew and became strong and increased in wisdom…and stature, in favor with God and men" (Lk 2:40, 52), spent significant time honing their trade down in Sepphoris, an urban center that was on one of Galilee's main highways and certainly offered more than enough work for a skilled builder.[43] If so, Jesus' upbringing would have introduced him not only to the world of rabbinic Judaism (there was a synagogue in Nazareth; Lk 4:16) but one of connected opportunity as well. From the crest of the high ridge on which Nazareth was built Jesus could gaze in the sweeping amphitheatre of the Jezreel Valley, a scene in which mighty men and women of his own people's past had tried to wrest redemption and freedom for Israel in centuries past (e.g., Barak, Deborah, Gideon, Saul, Elijah, Elisha and Josiah). The extent to which the memory of their deeds shaped his messianic awareness is a provocative discussion, but there can be no doubt that he came to see himself as fulfilling their combined role as Messiah. One sees that for him, oppression began with matters of the spirit and the heart.

Jesus was about thirty years old when he was baptized by John and began his public ministry. David was the same age when he became king (2 Sam 5:4), as were Levites (and, by extension, Rabbis) when they began to serve the spiritual needs of the people of Israel (Num 4:3). Scholars debate the length of time that passed between Jesus' baptism in the waters of the Jordan and his crucifixion in Jerusalem. While many posit a short ministry of one year or less (based on the pattern of the life-expectancy of the other messianic movements of his day)[44], the three Passover festivals mentioned in the Gospel of John, if they are sequential rather than simply episodic, suggest a ministry of nearly three years (cf. Jn 2:13; 6:4; 12:1). It is difficult to mesh the events of Jesus' life mentioned by John on chronological grounds with those recorded in the Synoptic Gospels (Matthew, Mark and Luke). Moreover, the

THE BAPTISM OF JESUS AND HIS SOJOURN IN THE WILDERNESS

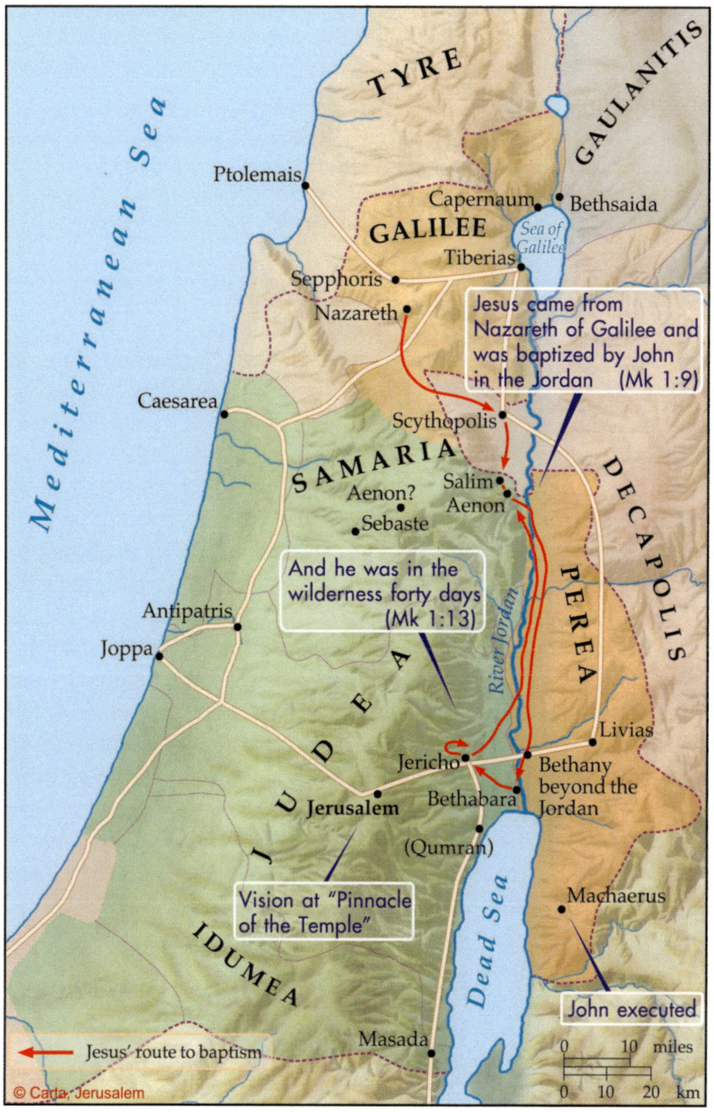

JESUS' MOVE FROM NAZARETH TO CAPERNAUM

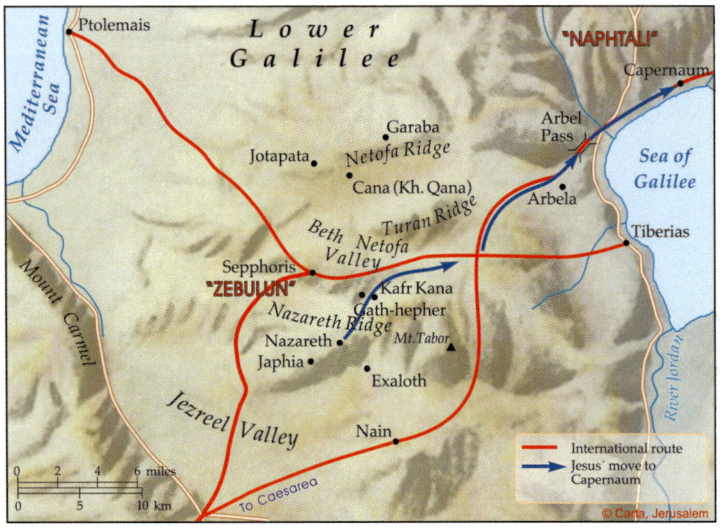

geographical clues offered by each gospel writer are also not always straightforward (it's a case of both too much information, and too little). Specific data of time and place (where Jesus did what, and when), the foundation of any connected narrative or historical reconstruction, are sufficiently incomplete so as to allow any number of supposed geographical and chronological sequences of the events of Jesus' life. A broad-stroke picture, however, is possible, taking into account that while the focus of Jesus' work was around the Sea of Galilee, certain trips to Jerusalem for the festivals is both reasonable and to have been expected.

After he was baptized Jesus withdrew immediately to the Judean wilderness, likely the arid region above Jericho, for forty days, into a landscape and for a period of time that echoed Israel's years of temptation and trial in "the great and terrible wilderness" of Sinai (cf. Deut 1:19). Here he resisted temptations by the devil to opt for various shortcuts to messiahship or methods of self-justified ease (Mt 4:1–11; Mk 1:12–13; Lk 4:1–13). In the end the devil withdrew, waiting "for an opportune time" (Lk 4:1–13). Anointed, tried and found worthy, Jesus entered a world of need.

He returned to Galilee, a political district governed by Herod Antipas that was home to an active Jewish population, though bisected by lively corridors of Hellenism. There he began to gather together a band of disciples. Eventually great crowds followed, even some who held positions of power and influence in Galilean and Judean society, but Jesus was most interested in choosing a special twelve ("those whom he himself wanted…that they might be with him"; Mk 3:13–14). This was a mixed band, representing in microcosm the hopes and dreams, socio-economic positions, suspicions and opportunities of Jewish Galilee (Mt 10:2–4; Mk 3:16–19; Lk 6:14–16). Nearly all were from the immediate region, calling the northern shore of the Sea of Galilee home. Though complete data for analysis lacks, it seems as though this was not a rag-tag bunch of down-and-outers who left situations in which they had nothing to gain in order to follow a local charismatic who promised the world. Yet each of them was searching for someone or something (certainly not all knew exactly what at first) who would redeem the times. Andrew, once a disciple of John the Baptist, got it right from the start: "We have found the Messiah" (Jn 1:41).

Sometime early on, after he had heard that his prophetic predecessor John the Baptist had been arrested, Jesus returned to his boyhood home of Nazareth (Mk 6:1–6; Lk 4:14–30; cf. Mt 4:12–13). He was already a man of some renown having done wondrous things in Capernaum and Cana (Lk 4:23; Jn 2:1–12; 4:46–54), a local-boy-done-good. Yet Jesus ran into trouble when he announced in the Nazareth synagogue that God was also in the business of blessing gentiles—folks such as the widow of Zarephath (a city between Tyre and Sidon; cf. 1 Kgs 17:8–24), the hated Syrian general Naaman (cf. 2 Kgs 5:1–14) and, by implication, the Hellenists and Romans surrounding and swallowing Nazareth in the first century A.D. (Lk 4:14–30). His ultra-nationalistic neighbors quickly cut him short by trying to toss him from the steep rocky mountainside that isolated their village from the imperialistic world of the Jezreel Valley below, down into the very arena in which God had worked His mighty deeds on behalf of Israel during the time of the Old Testament (Lk 4:16–30). Passing from their midst, Jesus moved down to Capernaum permanently (Lk 4:31; cf. Mt 9:1), fulfilling the promise of Isaiah, according to Matthew 4:12–16 (cf. Isa 9:1–7), that a great light would arise out of the land of Zebulun (where Nazareth was) and Naphtali (the homeland of Capernaum).

So leaving Nazareth behind, Jesus "withdrew to the sea with his disciples" (Mk 3:7). "The sea" was of course the Sea of Galilee (Mt 4:18; Mk 1:16), called the Sea of Tiberias in John 6:1 and 21:1 and the Lake of Gennesaret in Luke 5:1. In the first century A.D. the narrow shoreline of the Sea of Galilee was a crowded, bustling, rough-and-tumble arena where just about every kind of person that Jesus' disciples would someday meet around the rim of the vast Mediterranean Sea had already congregated, trying to wrest a decent living for themselves and their families in an unforgiving world. With a pleasant climate and fertile shoreline soil, the Sea of Galilee was a magnet for settlement and economic ventures. In addition, the major international highway carrying traffic through Galilee from the Mediterranean to desert caravan routes beyond Damascus tracked along its northern shore, from Tiberias to Bethsaida–Julius. Capernaum, Jesus' adopted hometown, lay along this route. Northeastward was Gaulanitis, an area of decidedly mixed population (Jewish and gentile) governed by Philip, the half-brother of Antipas. Bordering the sea on the southeast lay the Decapolis (Mt 4:25; Mk 5:20; 7:31)[45], a thoroughly Gentile district dominated by ten cities founded with the expressed purpose of disseminating a Greco-Roman world-view throughout the region and holding Rome's eastern frontier against armies beyond. The sea was large enough to contain a representative slice of everything the larger world had to offer, yet small enough so that news traveled quickly from one shore to another—news of a birth, a death, or a visitor who decided to make a town along the sea his new home, especially if that newcomer had a compelling personality and special powers.

Of the cities and villages around the Sea of Galilee, Capernaum was perhaps the one best suited to become the focal point of Jesus' ministry (cf. Mt 9:1). Archaeological evidence supports the idea that it was a center of fishing and, by implication, a variety of support trades. As many as eight boat docks or fishing piers dating to the first century A.D. have been found along a 2,500-foot stretch of shoreline at Capernaum, a larger number than were associated with Bethsaida–Julius, Hippus and Tiberias (the main lake cities of Gaulanitis, the Decapolis and Galilee respectively) combined. It seems also to have been a center of grain-mill production. The city, then, was a center of commerce, trade and, by extension, taxation. To protect Rome's interests in this easternmost town in Galilee, apparently one hundred Roman legionary troops were garrisoned at Capernaum, so that the residents of the town must have felt their occupation as acutely as did the people of Jerusalem. There was also a synagogue (in this case paid for by funds available to the centurion; Lk 7:1–10) indicating that a good portion of the Jewish residents of the city must have been religious, with scribes and Pharisees at hand (Mt 9:10–13; Mk 2:1–12; Lk 5:21). Jesus' relationship with the scribes and Pharisees was multi-dimensional,

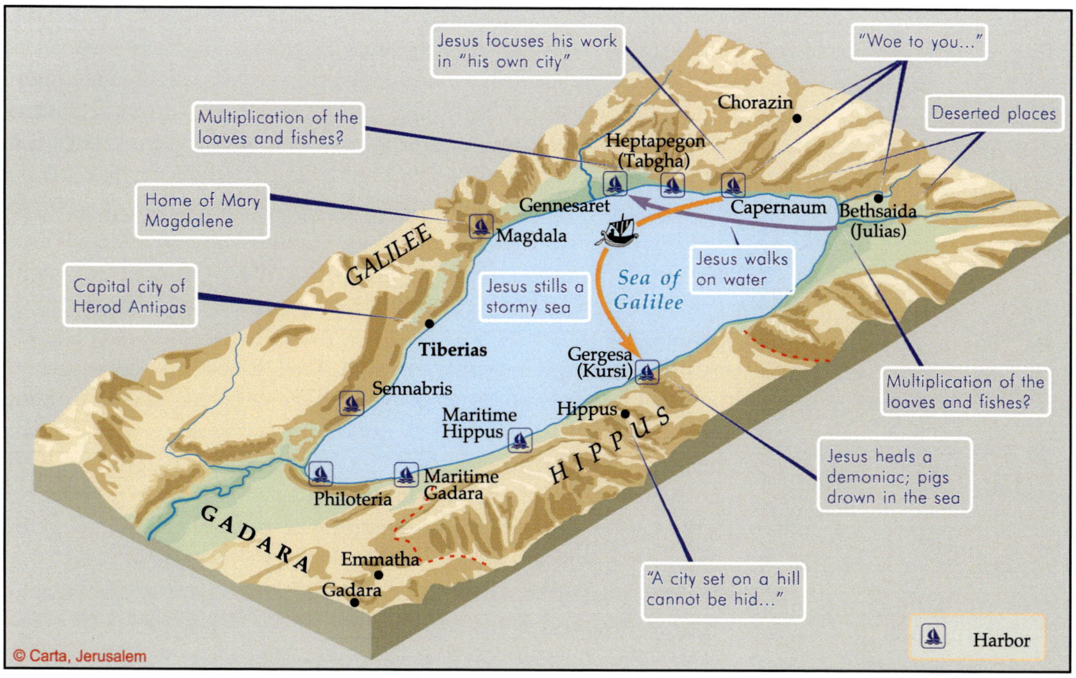

JESUS' TRAVELS AROUND THE SEA OF GALILEE

(below) This is a parable view—a hard path, thorns and plenty of good soil in which a seed might take root (Mk 4:1–9). These fields of the Beth Netopha Valley lie between Nazareth and Cana (Khirbet Qana), where Jesus must have walked often in the years of preparation for ministry. Here he had the opportunity to meet all sorts of people, from common village farmers to folks who exploited the regions' position as an international connector between the Sea of Galilee and the Mediterranean Sea. It was a rich testing ground of faith.

giving indication of his tendency to be both conservative and innovative in matters related to the world-view and personal behavior demanded by *Torah* (eg. Mt 5:17–48; 23:1–36). It might be supposed that Jesus' practical skills as a carpenter (*tekton*) were also in demand in a town as active as Capernaum.

So Jesus' ministry took shape around the sea, centered in his new home of Capernaum. It was here, as well as in Chorazin and Bethsaida, that Jesus would end up performing most of his miracles and, by implication, the residents would hear most often the good news of God's kingdom (the "gospel"; Gk. *euangelion*; cf. Isa 40:9). We can only imagine most of the specifics, as the Gospel writers fail to mention any of Jesus' visits to Chorazin and record only a very few of his activities in Bethsaida. Ironically, in the end much of what he said and did there was for naught, and Jesus sternly upbraided the residents of all three places for their lack of repentance even though they had witnessed the power of God face to face (Mt 11:20–24; Lk 10:10–15; cf. Mt 3:7–12).

While Jesus' ministry in the north carried him throughout Galilee and into the surrounding districts of Gaulanitis, the Decapolis and the region of Tyre, there is no mention in the Gospel accounts of him ever setting foot in the larger Hellenistic cities of the region: Tiberias, Hippus, Sepphoris, Scythopolis or others with similar names or demographics (he once visited "the region of Caesarea Philippi" but apparently not the city itself; cf. Mt 16:13). Some scholars have argued that Jesus' efforts to "keep kosher" (as a good rabbi would want to do) prevented him from entering places such as these that were ritually unclean (especially Tiberias, which was built over a cemetery; cf. *Ant.* xviii.36–38). Perhaps—but by avoiding the Greco-Roman cities of the region—Jesus (and the Gospel writers) also sent a message about the hollowness of the ways of the world: "All that stuff related to a Roman world view? It's not necessary for life. We can safely ignore it."

Jesus' miracles in and around Capernaum were dramatic and effective. So was his teaching, with authority (cf. Mk 1:21–22). The Gospel writers make a point to present Jesus' words and actions as things spoken and done with great intention. In teaching, Jesus often used traveling verbs: "Come" (Mt 11:28; Mk 6:31; Lk 9:23; 18:22; Jn 11:43); "Go" (Mt 5:41; 8:13; 9:6; 17:27; Mk 14:13; Lk 5:14; Jn 7:8); "Follow" (Mt 4:19; 9:9; Lk 9:23, 59; 18:22; Jn 10:4–5); "Send" (Mt 9:38; 10:16; Jn 20:21); "Walk" (Mt 9:5; 11:5; Lk 13:33; Jn 11:9–10). Like the prophets of old he recognized that the everyday act of moving about from one place to the other, usually by foot and over rough or rugged terrain, was a particularly apt image to speak about conditions of the human heart. Jesus' miracles of healing also echoed images from the heart from the Old Testament. He showed special concern for those who couldn't walk (Mt 8:5–13; 9:2–7; Mk 2:1–12; Jn 5:2–17) or see (Mt 9:27–31; 20:29–34; Lk 18:35–43; Jn 9:1–12), those whose bodies were marred by leprosy (Mt 8:1–4; Lk 17:11–19) or physical deformities (Mk 3:1–6; 5:25–34), or who were possessed by unclean spirits (Mt 8:16, 28–34; 9:32–34; 15:21–28; Mk 1:21–26; Lk 8:2). Most of the people whom Jesus healed had the kind of physical ailments that prophets of the Old Testament used as images to speak about problems of the heart (cf, Isa 6:9–10; 42:7, 16, 24; Jer 13:10), or that, according to provisions of *Torah,* made a person too unclean to stand before the LORD (e.g., Lev 13:1–14:57).[46] Jesus' healings met real human needs, but also sent a clear religious signal: if he had the power to heal physical ailments, he also had the power to heal the problem of sin (cf. Lk 5:17–26).

Jesus' first recorded miracle in Capernaum, driving a demon out of a man in the synagogue on the Sabbath, brought him instant publicity (Mk 1:21–28). He followed up that evening (after the

Students of the gospel gaze over the Plain of Gennesaret (Mt 14:34) from the heights of Arbel. The curve of the northwestern corner of the Sea of Galilee bends from Magdala to Capernaum, right. After his rejection in Nazareth this landscape became the adopted home of Jesus, and from its lively interplay of soil and water he drew his eager band of disciples. Launched from this shoreline to the vast beachhead of the Mediterranean, the world would never be the same.

Sabbath) by healing Peter's mother-in-law in her home, as well as others among "the whole city" that pressed about her door (Mk 1:29–34). It all offered an effective template around which his ministry would develop: public activities that challenged the existing power structures of the day, intermixed with prolonged attention to the masses, the *am ha-aretz* ("people of the land") who, "like sheep without a shepherd" (Mt 9:36), longed for direction and care. The next morning Jesus' disciples found him: "Everyone is looking for you," they said (Mk 1:35–37; cf. v. 45). Word was out. The skilled builder went to work on the kingdom of God.

As he went, Jesus seemed almost to go out of his way to be active on the Sabbath, the weekly day for spiritual (and physical) refreshment and rejoicing in creation, in *Torah* and in God's provision for life. "The Sabbath was made for man," Jesus declared, emphasizing its freeing, beneficial aspects, "not man for the Sabbath" (Mk 2:18–28). Most of the scribes and Pharisees would have agreed on the principle, although it was easy to debate details of practice. By action and by deed, Jesus sought to live in the freedom of *Torah*, God's word for right living (cf. Mt 5:17). But his attitude toward Sabbath observance was too liberal (or, generous) for many of his more scrupulous colleagues. None of the people whom Jesus healed on the Sabbath, for instance, had an imminent life-threatening condition (Mt 12:2–14; Mk 2:23–3:6; Lk 6:1–11; 13:10–17; 14:1–6; Jn 5:2–17; 7:19–24; 9:13–16), which, if they had, would have met exclusion requirements of rabbinic law.[47] Throughout, however, Jesus strove to get to the heart of the matter: one's attitude toward God and neighbor is the best indication of the real relevance of *Torah* in one's life (cf. the Sermon on the Mount, Mt 5:1–7:28; Lk 6:20–49). Many of the people of the land responded favorably, and a great multitude followed, from Galilee, Judea, Jerusalem, Idumea and Perea ("beyond the Jordan")—all areas with a dominant Jewish majority—but also folks from the vicinity of Tyre and Sidon, gentile-land (Mk 3:7–8). It was fertile soil, into which good seed fell and produced a hundredfold harvest (Mk 4:1–25).

On one occasion Jesus left Capernaum to "go over to the other side" of the lake (Mk 4:35). The indicator "to the other side" does not require that he traveled to a point exactly opposite the shoreline, but in effect only move from one of the political districts around the lake to another; this time he was apparently headed from Capernaum to the plain of Bethsaida or the part of Gaulanitis that edged the plain farther east. A fierce wind arose, pushing the small boat out to sea (Mk 4:36–41). Jesus stilled the storm (a marker linking him to the creative power of God), but the boat was blown into the area of the Decapolis. Though various early Church traditions locate his landing at Gadara or Gerasa, two prominent Decapolis cities south (and far south) of the lake, geographical common-sense places him at Gergesa (Kursi) just north of Hippus. There Jesus drove a legion of demons out of a man, probably a gentile, who was wholly possessed and socially non-functional. The man wanted to accompany Jesus back to Capernaum but was refused passage: his mission field was his own homeland (Mk 5:1–20). The next time Jesus came to the Decapolis he was met by a large crowd of people who were eagerly awaiting his return (Mk 7:31–37). Their comment? "[Jesus] has done all things well" (Mk 7:37).

Jesus returned to Capernaum and, after another period of teaching, healing and ministering, sent out his special twelve in pairs, two by two, into the towns and villages of Galilee (Mt 10:1–42; Mk 6:7–13; Lk 9:1–6). They went with his encouragement and instruction: don't go to the gentiles or to the Samaritans, but only to "the lost sheep of the house of Israel" (Mt 10:5–6). "Take only what is necessary. Reach as many people as possible. It won't be easy but there is no need to fear." It is impossible to know how long this first mission for the twelve lasted, but the conditions Jesus expected them to face echoed those that these same disciples, as Apostles ("sent ones"), would meet once they left the relative safety and security of Galilee for the "uttermost parts of the earth" (cf. Acts 1:8). Their discipleship would end up being costly; anyone who wanted to join Jesus' growing band might as well know that from the start (cf. Mt 10:24–42).

When the Apostles-in-training returned to Capernaum, they gave a good account of their work. (Mk 6:30; Lk 9:10). It hadn't been easy and so Jesus took them "to a secluded place" to rest and regroup (Mk 6:31; Lk 9:11). Church tradition marks the spot at Tabgha on the sea's northwestern shore, although some textual clues suggest that he was somewhere in Gaulanitis, northeast, instead (Lk 9:10-12). It was springtime, a glorious time to be out and about, and Passover was near (Mk 6:39; Jn 6:4). Setting aside his own agenda, Jesus spent the entire day with the multitudes and when it grew late he fed them all, some five thousand people, by a miraculous provision from one boy's lunch. This is the only miracle, except for the Resurrection, that is recorded in all four Gospels (Mt 14:13–21; Mk 6:33–44; Lk 9:12–17; Jn 6:1–14). Perhaps that says something about the power of the multitudes on the call of the Messiah.

After feeding the five thousand, Jesus needed time by himself and so sent his disciples back across the lake in the boat, late in the evening. A sudden spring-time storm hit the lake, blowing strongly. The direction they were sailing depends on the location of the prior episode; the geographical clues are as choppy as was the water during their voyage. Map-makers remain adrift; Jesus at least rescued the men in the boat, walking to them on the crashing waves (Mt 14:22–33; Mk 6:47–52; Jn 6:16–21). His disciples were utterly astonished: it was one thing to still the stormy sea; it was quite another to walk out into the liquid jaws of the Cosmic Deep and trample Death under one's feet. All came ashore at Gennesaret, on the northwestern shore of the sea (Mt 14:34; Mk 6:53), the waters calm, the disciples likely in the stupor of post-traumatic shock, and another crowd of people, eager, wide-eyed and innocent, waiting to touch their Messiah. Was there no rest for the righteous?

They were back in Galilee again, and Jesus was approached

THE TRANSFIGURATION

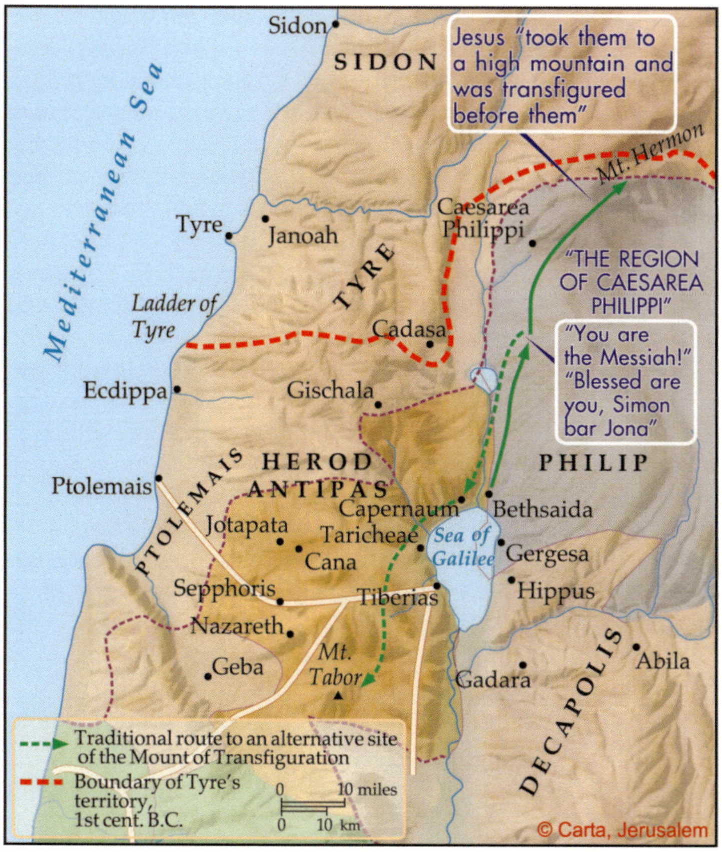

by a contingent of scribes and Pharisees from Jerusalem who took exception with his approach to *Torah*. With opposition among his fellow rabbis growing Jesus decided that it was time to make a bold move and so he and his disciples traveled first into the region of Tyre and Sidon, then around and over to the Decapolis. Here Jesus' disciples were clearly out of their comfort zone (Mt 15:21–28; Mk 7:24–37). From the Decapolis it was over to Magadan (Mt 15:39) and Dalmanutha (Mk 8:10), two places otherwise unknown in ancient sources (perhaps both are names for the same site). Jesus and his disciples then reentered Bethsaida where he restored sight to a blind man (Mk 8:22–26). As was his pattern up to now, he asked the man who was healed to keep it quiet. But things were about to take a dramatically new course.

From Bethsaida Jesus and his disciples traveled north toward the *polis* of Caesarea Philippi (Panias), nestled against the southern end of Mount Hermon. Here a true Roman city was taking shape, with abundant vegetation fed by a powerful spring (a major source of the Jordan River) issuing out of a large cave at the base of a mammoth limestone cliff. The city was dedicated both to the Greco-Roman god of nature, Pan, and to the divine Caesar Augustus (now dead; Philip's father, Herod the Great, had built a classical Roman temple to Augustus in the vicinity). Herod Philip elevated the place to the capital of his tetrarchy, creating an atmosphere that would make any Rome-oriented traveler from the greater Mediterranean world feel right at home. It was to the region of Caesarea Philippi, far both in terms of mileage and distance of the heart from Jewish communities in Jerusalem and in the vicinity of the Sea of Galilee, that Jesus brought his disciples to ask, "Who do people say the Son of Man is?" (Mt 16:13). Son of Man was perhaps Jesus' favorite title, and indicated his messianic, eschatological self-awareness (cf. Dan 7:13–14; 1 Enoch 48:2–7; 62:7; cf. 2 Esdras 13:1–58). It was Peter (*Petros*) who answered, "You are the Messiah, the Son of the Living God" (Mt 16:14–16). Jesus followed up with his first and most significant mention of the church, an institution that would be built on "this rock" (Gk. *Petra*; Mt 16:17–19; cf. Mt 18:17, the only other time the word church occurs in the Gospels). While theologians have long debated the intent of Jesus' use of the term "rock," it remains interesting that his reference was made in the vicinity of the great cliff of Caesarea Philippi, the "toe" of the massive rock of Mount Hermon, a massif made of the kind of hard limestone that provides the best water resources, building materials and soil of all of the rocks of the land of Israel; in other words, a natural resource in which one can find strength, security and everything necessary for life, even in an otherwise hostile and pagan environment—just like the church should be. It was a moment of great expectation. Jesus followed with a jarring dose of reality, the first of three predictions of his own Passion (cf. Mt 17:22–23; 20:17–19). And if that wasn't enough, he called for a jarring decision from those among his disciples who might want to follow: "If anyone wishes to come after me, he must deny himself and take up his cross and follow me" (Mt 16:24). Was *this* to be the way of the Messiah?

Six days later Jesus took his inner three, Peter, James and John, up to a high mountain where he was transfigured before them. Moses and Elijah, the two greatest prophets of old, also appeared, shining like the sun (Mt 17:1–4; Mk 9:2–4; Lk 9:28–31). While the dominant Byzantine tradition (Origen and Cyril of Jerusalem) placed the Transfiguration on Mount Tabor, a prominent peak (elev. 1,929 ft.) on the northeastern corner of the Jezreel Valley conveniently located on the pilgrim route between Nazareth and Capernaum, an alternative voice (Eusebius) suggested that the location may have been on Mount Hermon (elev. 9,233 ft.). Jesus, after all, was already in the vicinity, and Mount Hermon had the advantage of being northeast of the Rift Valley, the same side of the Jordan River on which Moses and Elijah had spent their final moments on earth before being ushered into the presence of God (Deut 34:1–6; 2 Kgs 2:7–12). High mountains and prophetic revelation go hand-in-hand in the biblical text (cf. Ex 19:10–20:21; 1 Kgs 19:9–18; 2 Pet 1:16–19), and so it was apparently here that Jesus, already in post-resurrection splendor, again heard the anointing-call of God (Mt 17:5; cf. Mk 9:7; Lk 9:35; Mt 3:17; Mk 1:11; Lk 2:14; 3:22). Jesus was the object of attention, but the intent of the matter was for his disciples. It was a pivotal moment; there was no turning back. Jesus "resolutely set his face to go to Jerusalem" (Lk 9:51).

Jesus called Peter for a second time somewhere along the northern shore of the Sea of Galilee (Jn 21:1–23). This image, at the Primacy of Peter church, seals the moment.

JESUS' EARLY TRIPS TO JERUSALEM ACCORDING TO THE GOSPEL OF JOHN

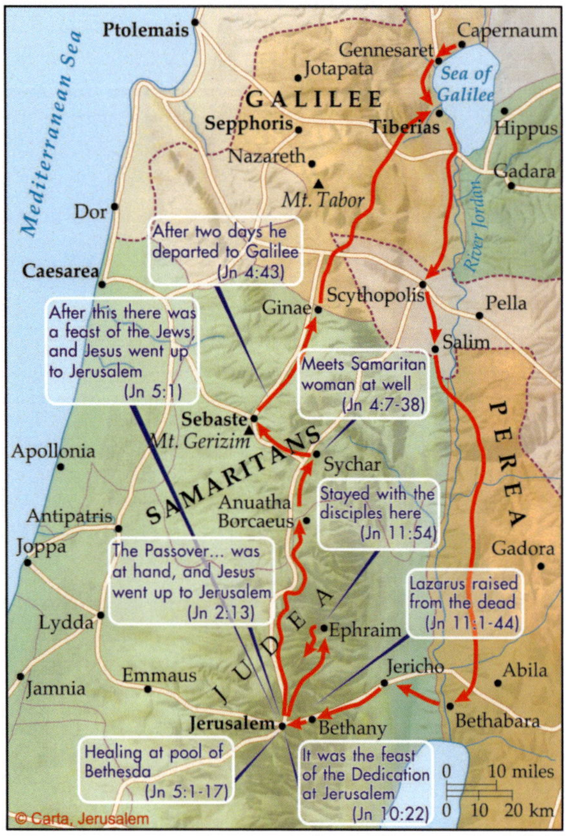

Mount Hermon was the farthest point from Jerusalem to which Jesus traveled in his years of public ministry. He was there, likely, sometime in the summertime, nine months before the Passover of his crucifixion. And so began his final journey, a nine-month circuitous march touching every area (except for the region of Tyre) which he had visited before, his words and actions building to a climax, his crowd of followers growing like a train of captives ascending on high (cf. Ps 68:18; Eph 4:7–8), in one grand Triumphal Entry climaxing in a procession over the top of the Mount of Olives the Sunday before Passover. Jesus did make a few side-journeys to Jerusalem on the way, for Succoth and Hanukkah (the festivals of Booths and Dedication; Jn 7:2–10:39) and to raise Lazarus from the dead (Jn 11:1–54), but these don't detract from the force of the main line of his march.

Jesus had been in Jerusalem at least twice before, once when he met Nicodemus, a member of the Sanhedrin who became a secret follower of the Galilean rabbi (Jn 3:1–21; 7:50–52; 19:38–42) and once when he healed a man at the Pool of Bethesda who had been ill for thirty-eight years (Jn 5:1–17). In between these two visits to Jerusalem Jesus and his disciples had returned to Galilee via Samaria where he stopped in the village of Sychar beneath Mount Gerizim (Jn 4:1–6). He ended up staying two days, and many Samaritans came to believe that he was the Messiah, including the outcast woman at the well, a person as opposite the social spectrum from Nicodemus as Jesus' disciples could imagine (Jn 4:7–43).

These were his earlier journeys to Jerusalem. Now from Mount Hermon as Jesus headed south, with the Holy City and a rendezvous at the cross in sight, he announced his destiny again (Mk 9:31). A messiah resigned to suffering and death was not on the first-century radar screen, and the disciples had little clue what he was talking about (Mk 9:32; cf. Mt 17:23).

Jesus apparently spent the bulk of his time that last winter in Perea, across the Jordan. Here we can reasonably place the events and teachings of Luke's "Special Section" (9:51–18:30), a narrative flow not included in the other Gospels. Historically Perea was a staging ground for armies or people groups wanting to infiltrate or conquer the land of Israel (e.g., Joshua, Eglon, Jephthah, Tobiah, and the Ammonites, Moabites, Midianites and others generally), and here Jesus went to get ready for his final climb to Jerusalem. He had left Galilee behind to move into position on the Holy City, and because Perea was an area of strong Jewish settlement and, like Galilee, under the political authority of Herod Antipas ("that fox"; Lk 13:32), Jesus was able to continue to build momentum unabated. One senses a real urgency in his movements and teachings, especially here, as the months and weeks grew short (Lk 12:4–5, 35, 37; 13:33; 14:27; 18:29–30). Then, as winter turned to spring and the great Passover freedom festival drew nigh, Jesus announced his coming Passion a third time (Lk 18:31–33).

Now for the final assault on the Holy City. Jesus and his disciples crossed the Jordan River opposite Jericho, at the place of his baptism, where at the command of Moses Joshua and the children of Israel had entered the Promised Land, and where Elisha, endowed with the double-spirit of Elijah, stepped into a world of need (Josh 3:1–17; 2 Kgs 2:13–14; Mt 3:13–17; Jn 1:19–34). Then they made their way through the parched nothingness of the southern Rift Valley to Jericho, an oasis of Roman imperial might awash in an arid sea. Here royal palaces of the Maccabees, Herod the Great and Archelaus still set the tone for the region, shouting the opulent "can-do" of the Empire. Here Jesus met the blind beggar Bartimaeus and the opportunistic tax collector Zaccheus; both responded to his call (Lk 18:35–19:10).

So Jesus climbed one last time, approaching Jerusalem from the east. King David had fled down this route to escape the *coup d'etat* of Absalom, then retraced his steps to Jerusalem to receive back his kingdom (2 Sam 15:23, 30; 16:1, 5, 13; 19:15, 18, 40). When the Babylonians destroyed the first Temple the Glory of the God of Israel left Jerusalem and stood over the Mount of Olives as the people of Jerusalem were hurled into exile, then returned from the east to fill the rebuilt Temple (Ezek 9:3; 10:18–19; 11:22–23; 43:1–5). Isaiah foresaw the LORD entering Jerusalem from the east, and called for the way to be prepared for His advance on the city (Isa 40:3–5).

Jesus and his disciples climbed to Bethany (*el-'Azariyeh*), a village on the eastern slope of the Mount of Olives a little less than two miles from Jerusalem (cf. Jn 11:18). This was Jesus' Jerusalem-based home, and he apparently stayed there whenever he was in the area (Mt 21:17; Mk 11:11; Lk 10:38–42; 21:37). Here he ate his last Sabbath meal with his disciples and some close friends, including Martha, Mary (a Mary other than his mother or Mary Magdalene) and Lazarus, whom he had raised from the dead there six weeks before (Jn 12:1–2; cf. Jn 11:1–46). It was six days before the Passover. Jesus spent the entire Sabbath in Bethany and the next day, the first and busiest business day of the week, brought his grand Triumphal Entry to a climax (Mt 21:1–9; Mk 11:1–10; Lk 19:28–44; Jn 12:12–19; cf. Zech 9:9). The expectations of the crowds were for salvation ("Hosanna!" "Save us, now!"), but many or all surely thought in terms of a political-religious mix.

Jesus spent most of his time the next few days in and around the temple, returning to Bethany to spend each night with his closest circle of supporters and friends (Mt 21:17; Mk 11:19; Lk 21:37). His time had finally arrived, and he held nothing back. He even turned over the tables of the money-changers in anger over the financial excesses of the temple hierarchy (Mt 21:12–16). Throughout was a long series of teachings—some upbraiding, others more gentle—about the need to get ready for the coming kingdom of God (Mt 21:28–25:46). The climax, sure to win enemies, was his lengthy diatribe against the scribes and Pharisees, said not because of what they taught (Jesus recognized the rightness of Pharisaic authority; Mt 23:2–3), but because of what they did ("they preach, but do not practice" (Mt 23:3). Somewhere toward the end of the week Jesus made preparations to celebrate the Passover meal with his disciples (Mt 26:17–29; Mk 14:12–25; Lk 22:7–23; Jn 13:1–17:26). Partway through the meal Judas Iscariot excused himself (he had previously arranged to sell Jesus to the Temple authorities for thirty pieces of silver, the *Torah* price for a slave accidentally gored by an ox; Mt 26:14–16; Mk 14:10–11; Lk 22:3–6; cf. Ex 21:32). Judas' motives certainly were political; ironically, he was perhaps the first of the disciples to try to come to terms with the reality that Jesus' kingdom was not aimed at driving Rome from Judea and Galilee. While two thousand years of Christian Western civilization have thoroughly vilified Judas as the archetype of sanctimonious hypocrisy (or worse), as a dark, bulbous Shylock driven by avarice and misguided self-zeal, it is likely that he was simply disillusioned, feeling that it was not he but Jesus, so full of promise, who had betrayed the cause. Jesus knew what was going on, but the other disciples were largely clueless (Mt 26:21–25; Mk 14:17–21; Lk 22:21–23; Jn 18:4).

After the meal Jesus and his disciples left the city, crossed the Kidron Valley and started to climb the Mount of Olives. The hour was late, and as the disciples all slept, Jesus faced the certainty of his impending death with God (Mt 26:36–46). There he was betrayed by one of his own disciples, arrested, and hauled before Caiaphas in what was to be the first of several trials over the next few hours (Mt 26:47–56; Mk 14:43–52; Lk 22:47–53; Jn 18:1–11). It was during Jesus' hearing before Caiaphas that Peter, always out in front, denied three times knowing Jesus (Mt 26:57–75; Mk 14:53–72; Lk 22:54–71; Jn 18:12–27). Caiaphas accused Jesus of blasphemy, a crime deserving death by stoning according to Jewish law.[48] The power to execute, however, lay in the hands of Rome (Jn 18:31), and so Caiaphas sent Jesus to Pilate (Mt 27:1–14; Mk 15:1–5; Lk 23:1–5). Not sure of the situation and unwilling to risk further exacerbating an already tenuous relationship with his Jewish subjects, Pilate shipped Jesus the Galilean off to Herod Antipas, who was in Jerusalem for Passover. Antipas was glad to finally see Jesus face-to-face, hoping that this "magic man of Galilee" would put on quite a show, but Jesus remained silent. Antipas arrayed Jesus in mock tribute, then sent him back to Pilate where he was tortured by the Roman soldiers before being sentenced to death by crucifixion (Mt 27:15–31; Mk 15:6–20; Lk 23:17–25; Jn 18:28–19:15).

So Jesus, beaten, scourged, mocked and already half-dead, made his last journey from the judgment hall of Pilate through Jerusalem's crowded streets then outside the city to a place of crucifixion, Golgotha, the Place of the Skull (Mt 27:32; Mk 15:21; Lk 23:26–32; Jn 19:17). His *Via Dolorosa* bore no directional relation to the street of the same name today or to its Stations of the Cross which represent a pious accretion of faithful memories over the centuries. Almost certainly, however, the crucifixion took place within, or very near to, ground occupied by Jerusalem's Church of the Holy Sepulcher. This was a known spot of crucifixion, just outside the city wall and adjacent to an area of tombs dating to the first century. Here Jesus was crucified between two thieves, nailed to a tree with his feet just off the ground and his face nearly eye-level with his accusers and passers-by, stark naked, intentionally humiliated and left to the abuses of the hot sun and of flies and insects drawn to blood, wild animals and birds hungry for a meal.[49]

And the people—some mocking, others feigning indifference, and yet a few unable to draw themselves from the final horrifying moments of their loved one (Mt 27:33–56; Mk 15:22–41; Lk 23:33–49; Jn 19:18–30). Sometimes it took days to die. Only a few women were faithful to the end, among them Mary Magdalene from whom Jesus had cast a demon, Mary the mother of James, Joses and Salome, and his own mother (Mt 27:55; Jn 19:25–27; cf. Lk 8:2). Mercifully, death came in just a few hours (cf. Mt 27:45).

There was little time to prepare the body properly for burial. Nicodemus helped by bringing myrrh and aloes for a kind of hasty mummification (Mt 27:57–61; Jn 19:31–42). Both Joseph and Nicodemus risked becoming ritually impure by the venture. Within hours, according to the chronology of the Gospel of John, they would eat the Passover meal, celebrating again redemption from Egypt, looking again for freedom from Rome, wondering. How the Marys spent the night can only be imagined.

The next day was the Sabbath. No one could possibly come to the tomb (Lk 23:56). But the next morning Mary Magdalene and Mary the mother of James, Joses and Salome, did come—early—with spices to anoint their Messiah for burial. There was no need. The tomb was empty. Jesus had risen, just like he said (Mt 28:1–10; Mk 16:1–11; Lk 24:1–12; Jn 20:1–18; cf. Mt 16:21; 17:22–23; 20:18–19). The women told Peter and John, who had to come and see for themselves. Then word began to spread, first to the eleven disciples, then beyond.

That afternoon, Jesus encountered two men walking to the village of Emmaus and to them he "explained the things concerning himself in all the Scriptures" (Lk 24:13–35; cf. v. 27; Mk 16:12–13). They added their testimony of the risen Lord to that of Simon Peter, and then to others as Jesus made himself known to his disciples in Jerusalem (Mt 28:16–17; Mk 16:14; Lk 24:36–49; Jn 20:19–29; cf. 1 Cor 15:3–8). Jesus also appeared to some of his disciples on the shore of the Sea of Galilee who had gone fishing with Peter (Jn 21:1–23), and he called them, again (cf. Lk 5:1–11). He wasn't about to let his mission die.

Forty days after his resurrection Jesus met the eleven remaining disciples on the Mount of Olives. Encouraging them with the promise that they would receive the power of the Holy Spirit, Jesus also commissioned them to be his witnesses "in Jerusalem, and in all Judea and Samaria, and even to the most remote part of the earth" (Acts 1:1–8). And with that, the disciples had a choice: either walk down the backside of the Mount of Olives, retrace their steps through the Judean Wilderness to Jericho, head north and return to what promised to be a secure and profitable future around the shore of the Sea of Galilee, glad for their experiences with Jesus but ready to get back to real life. Or, follow Jesus' footsteps down the western slope of the mount, cross the Kidron Valley and climb into Jerusalem, carrying Jesus' message to a world waiting for consolation and redemption (cf. Lk 2:25, 38). And this they did. Eventually Jesus' followers took the name "Christians" (Acts 11:26), anointed ones. Like their Lord, they were filled with his image to carry the grace and truth of God to a waiting world in need (cf. Jn 1:17).

THE ROAD TO EMMAUS

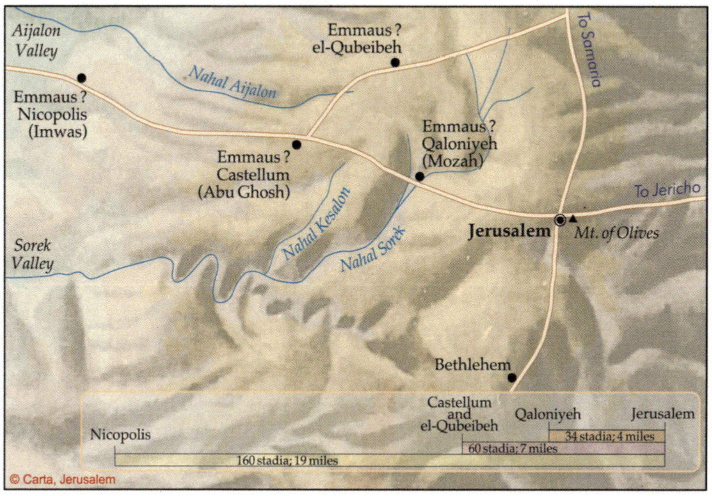

PONTIUS PILATE

Pontius Pilate, who held the Roman political office of prefect of Judea from A.D. 26–36, was by most reasonable estimates someone who was part beholden, part butcher, part anti-Semite, and part man of sheer personal expediency. Pilate burst onto the scene of Judea with the stage filled by a host of veteran actors already following multiple scripts, none of which included lines he was fit to read. It was a toxic mix. Before the curtain fell he was yanked off stage having made it messier by virtue of his being there. Attempts to redeem Pilate as a fellow who was well meaning but misunderstood, genuine but somehow misguided, or an honest seeker of truth who just didn't push his curiosity quite far enough largely fall on deaf ears. Let them lie. When ancient sources as diverse in opinion as Philo, Josephus and the Gospels all point in the same direction, it's proper to call a spade a spade.

Rome's decision to appoint Pontius Pilate as prefect of Judea was part of a sequence of events that slowly pulled the region toward the center of Rome's orbit of control. After Pompey entered Jerusalem in 63 B.C. and brought the Jewish Hasmonean kingdom to an inglorious end, Rome initially tried to maintain control of Judea by backing cooperative members of the disposed Hasmonean royal family, principly Hyrcanus II who as high priest had been a legitimate claimant to the Jewish throne. Hyrcanus proved to be ineffective (most of his subjects despised collaborators) and so in the summer of 40 B.C. the Senate instead appointed a local strongman, Herod the Great, as client king. Herod was a man of excess but at least had the presence of mind and sleight of hand to keep a lid on things that would cause Caesar undue concern. His son Archelaus, who inherited Judea, Idumea and Samaria in 4 B.C., was beneficiary of Herod's iron-fisted will but at eighteen was too young to know how to add the necessary political and diplomatic finesse to make it all work. Within ten years Archelaus had offended virtually every element of the local population and so in AD 6 Caesar Augustus banished him to the northern reaches of Gaul and created a new province out of the region (*Ant.* xvii.200–247, 339–353; xviii.1).

Augustus had several options. Provinces within the empire that were stable and generally free from threat were placed under the control of the Roman Senate. Others—and these were the majority in the empire—faced the possibility of ongoing unrest from either external or internal threats and so remained under the direct control of the emperor. Of these Imperial Provinces the more critical, such as Syria, were governed by men of senatorial rank (*legatus Augusti pro praetore*) and supplied with crack legionary troops. Others, including Egypt, Cappadocia, Sardinia and Judea, were placed under the authority of equestrians (*equites*; "knights"), men of proven military ability who were still climbing the ladder of success within the imperial system. When Archelaus was dismissed Judea became a province of this type but with the apparent understanding that the governor of Syria held veto power over internal matters. It was a hook that would come in handy later. With Augustus' decision the people of Judea (including Idumea and Samaria) came under the heavy fist of direct Roman rule (*Ant.* xvii.354–355; *War* ii.117–118).

Until the reign of Emperor Claudius (A.D. 41–54), the governors of imperial equestrian provinces were called prefects (*praefectus*), a term that was proper for seasoned military officers who commanded five hundred to one thousand troops. Only after the reign of Claudius was the title "prefect" replaced by the more familiar term "procurator," designating the chief financial officer of a province. Evidence for the use of "prefect" as the proper title for the early governors of Judea comes chiefly in a broken inscription found in archaeological excavations in Caesarea mentioning Pilate as *[praef] ectus Iuda[ea]e*.[50] Josephus' references to Pilate as "procurator of

PROVINCES OF THE ROMAN EMPIRE, A.D. 117

Judea" appear to be anachronistic (cf. *Ant.* xviii.55; *War* ii.169); the writers of the Gospels preferred the more generic title "governor" (*hegemon*) for all higher Roman officials, including the prefect, who served in the region (Mt 27:2; Mk 13:9; Lk 2:2; 3:1; 20:20).

The prefects of Judea typically were appointed and dismissed by Caesar himself. Until the reign of Claudius, all were natives of Italy, a pattern which probably helped to ensure that the new province would be governed by men known by, and particularly loyal to, the emperor. Their duties were directly related to enforcing Rome's will. High on each prefect's job description was control of the auxiliary troops, which for Judea were drawn from the local Hellenistic populations of Caesarea and Sebaste (*Ant.* xx.173–178). If the prefect of Judea needed additional military help he had to appeal to the governor of Syria for access to the legions. The prefect was also the highest judicial authority in the province, holding the exclusive right to enforce capital punishment (*War* ii.117). Additionally, he was responsible for the province's financial affairs, which included levying taxes, implementing the corvée and minting coins. Rome also allowed the prefect to appoint and dispose of high priests, a right necessary for maintaining a firm line of control in the province but something that was a constant show of humiliation for the Jews; over time it further politicized the temple hierarchy already given to power plays and expediency. As a corollary, until the end of the governorship of Pilate the prefect also administered the use of the high-priestly vestments, an act that had practical ramifications as large as its symbolism (*Ant.* xviii.90–95). Any one of these several duties brought the prefect into direct conflict with the powers and people of Judea, and to be effective he had to be a man with refined skills of diplomacy and coercion.

PONTIUS PILATE, PREFECT OF JUDEA, A.D. 26–36

Judea's first three prefects apparently strove for a relatively favorable relationship with their Jewish subjects. These were Coponius (A.D. 6–9?), Marcus Ambivulus (A.D. 9?–12) and Annius Rufus (A.D. 12–15). The fourth, Valerius Gratus (A.D. 15–26), had a mixed record. During his long term in office Gratus dismissed and/or appointed no less than five high priests, including Annas, who was fired not long after Gratus took office, and Annas' son-in-law Caiaphas, whom Gratus appointed toward the end of his tenure (cf. Jn 18:13). Caiaphas remained in power throughout the term of Pilate, leading some to suggest, certainly correctly, that at the very least the high priest had gained the trust of the Roman authorities. Likely Rome found Caiaphas a convenient tool to foster Jewish loyalties to the empire, or at least someone who wouldn't rock the boat in the matter.

Next after Gratus was Pontius Pilate (A.D. 26–36). Like his immediate predecessors, Pilate appears to have been a native of central Italy. The family name Pontius has been traced, with some likelihood, to the hilly region of Samnium in south-central Italy, 130 miles east of Rome. The specific name Pilate is much more rare; none of its supposed meanings ("armed with a javelin," "bald" and "shaggy") are of any help in shedding light on the origin or character of the man. Pilate was appointed prefect of Judea after what must have been a fairly noticeable career in the equestrian orders of the Roman military system.

Some scholars have suggested that Pilate's appointment, which should have been made by Tiberius alone, was influenced by Sejanus, the powerful chief of Caesar's Praetorian Guard.[51] Sejanus was a known proponent of anti-Semitic policies in Rome and it is likely that he was attracted to Pilate—and vice versa—because the latter fostered the same tendencies. Philo, an Alexandrian Jew, wrote freely and bluntly of the excesses of Pilate, his contemporary. According to Philo, Pilate was a man "with a very inflexible disposition, merciless and most obstinate," possessed by "most ferocious passions" and someone who was widely feared because of his "corruption, acts of insolence, rapine behavior, habit of insulting people, cruelty, continual murders of people untried and uncondemned, and his never ending, gratuitous and most grievous inhumanity"—a list of seven deadly sins if there ever was one.[52]

Having taken up residency in Caesarea, Pilate wasted no time in offending the Jews under his charge. His first act was to transfer the army from Caesarea to Jerusalem in the wintertime, a move that makes no sense given the local weather patterns other than to allow Pilate to brazenly show his hand as to who exactly was in charge of the Holy City (*Ant.* xviii.55–59). The army arrived in Jerusalem replete with royal ensigns bearing the image of Tiberius, a clear affront to Jewish law and religious sensibilities. After a tense six-day test of wills in which the Jews insisted that if necessary they would submit to martyrdom for the cause, Pilate pulled his army back, publically humiliated. In a similar incident related by Philo,[53] the Jewish leadership of Jerusalem appealed directly to Caesar Tiberius in Rome to force Pilate to remove donor-inscribed golden shields decorating his palace in Jerusalem. Tiberius sided with the Jews; Pilate, called on the carpet in both Rome and Judea, didn't wear it well.

Sometime later—Josephus doesn't mention when—Pilate got into trouble for what probably appeared to him as a simple and necessary improvement in Jerusalem's infrastructure: lengthening

THE ARREST, TRIALS AND CRUCIFIXION OF JESUS—A POSSIBLE SEQUENCE

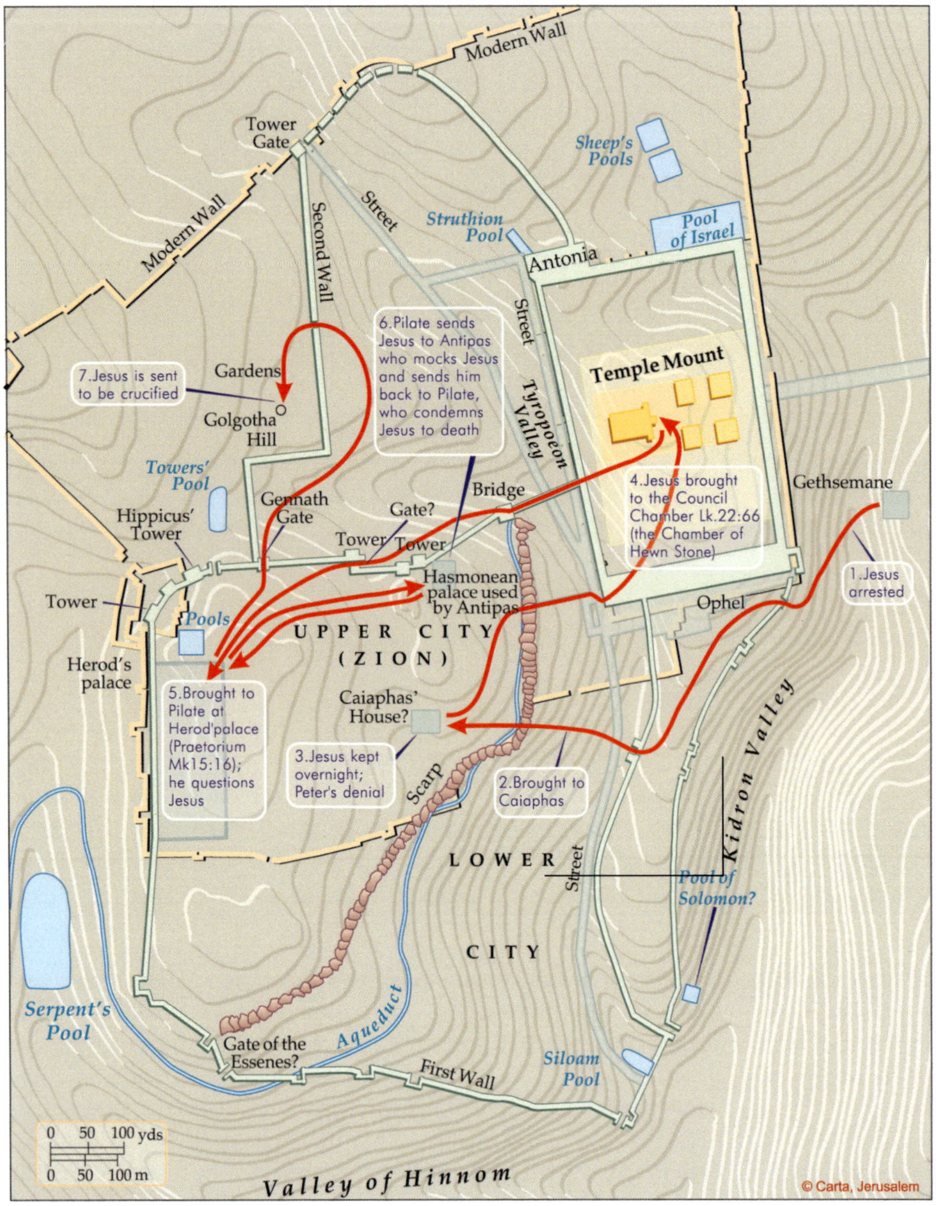

the Hasmonean and Herodian aqueduct that brought water into the city from the hills of Hebron (*Ant.* xviii.60–62). His offense was that he paid for the project out of (extorted) temple funds, money that had been designated "*Corban*" ("devoted;" cf. Mt 7:11) and so was restricted for sacred use. Pilate responded to the protest by having his soldiers, dressed as commoners, mingle and kill at will in the unsuspecting crowd. The incident is similar to one recorded by Luke in which Pilate "mixed the blood of Galileans with their sacrifices" (Lk 13:1–3). The particulars of this event are unstated but easily imagined—if asked, Pilate probably would have called it insurrection. He had no authority in Galilee, but when a number of Galileans ran afoul of his will while on a holy pilgrimage to Jerusalem, Pilate's response was true to form.

Somewhere in the middle of Pilate's lengthy term of office Jesus of Nazareth made his final pilgrimage to Jerusalem. His entrance down the Mount of Olives the Sunday morning before Passover was dramatic—triumphant, even—as shouts of "Hosanna (Save, now!)" and "Blessed is the king who comes in the name of the LORD!" echoed into the city (Mt 21:9; Lk 19:38). Jerusalem was already crowded with pilgrims getting ready for the Passover, the Jewish freedom festival, and so according to pattern Pilate likely sent extra troops into Jerusalem to offset any populist tendencies that might give rise to expressions of freedom that threatened Rome (cf. *War* i.88–89; ii.8–13, 223–227; v.238–247). He himself would also typically come to the city for the festival to keep a personal watch on things. But this year the week before Passover started badly for Pilate—a report no doubt reached his desk that the crowds couldn't even wait for the holiday to begin before clamoring for some rabbi from Galilee to overthrow the government.

Certain members of the temple hierarchy also wanted Jesus gone. The Gospels say "from envy" (Mt 27:18; Mk 15:10)—apparently Jesus was attracting too large a following—but many members of Jerusalem's priesthood, especially Sadducees comfortable with the *status quo*, had no patience for movements clamoring for revolutionary change. Thanks to Judas Iscariot's inside job, Jesus was taken off the streets quickly and quietly (Mt 26:47–56; Mk 14:43–52; Lk 22:47–62; Jn 18:1–16). The high priest Caiaphas, responsible for a complex weave of political and religious interests in Judea, Galilee and throughout the Diaspora, delivered Jesus to Pilate on the crime of blasphemy punishable by the sentence of death (Mt 26:57–27:2; Mk 14:53–15:1; Lk 22:63–23:1; Jn 18:12–27). Rome alone held the authority to execute (cf. Jn 18:31).

Pilate had no interest in internal Jewish religious matters unless they touched on issues of security and control—he probably resented being drawn into what he considered the quirky controversies of the Jews—and so the charge against Jesus was given with the appropriate nuance: "We found this man misleading our nation, forbidding us to give tribute to Caesar and saying that he himself is the Messiah, a king" (Lk 23:2). Thus drawn into the affair, Pilate interrogated Jesus over his purported role and vision of a Jewish kingdom. Pilate preferred the direct approach, and was immediately frustrated by what he saw as an impossible case. If he passed sentence of execution, he risked another riot by the crowds who last he heard were still looking for the Messiah. But if he turned him loose, he risked further alienating the local religious authorities who wanted Jesus dead. Hearing that Jesus was a Galilean, Pilate shipped him across town to Herod Antipas, who also had come to Jerusalem for the Passover. The tetrarch of Galilee was not opposed to seeing Jesus; he had already executed John the Baptist (Mt 14:1–12). Antipas grilled Jesus well, but the prisoner maintained his silence. Without extradition to Galilee there was little Antipas could do other than taunt Jesus and send him back to Pilate (Lk 23:6–12).

It was time to finish the case, but in doing so Pilate seems to have had a little fun in the process by trying to undercut the claim of Jesus' accusers while picking away at the absurdity of the perpetual political-religious mix of Judaism that had given him such trouble in the past. And so Pilate announced his decision, wholly unexpected by everyone: "I find no fault in him" (Lk 23:13–16; Jn 18:38). By throwing Jesus back to the multitudes from which he came, Pilate apparently thought that he could provoke another insurrection (this one Jesus-led), then have the excuse to crush once and for all the seething and arrogant hope of an independent Jewish

THE AQUEDUCT TO JERUSALEM
1ST CENTURY A.D.

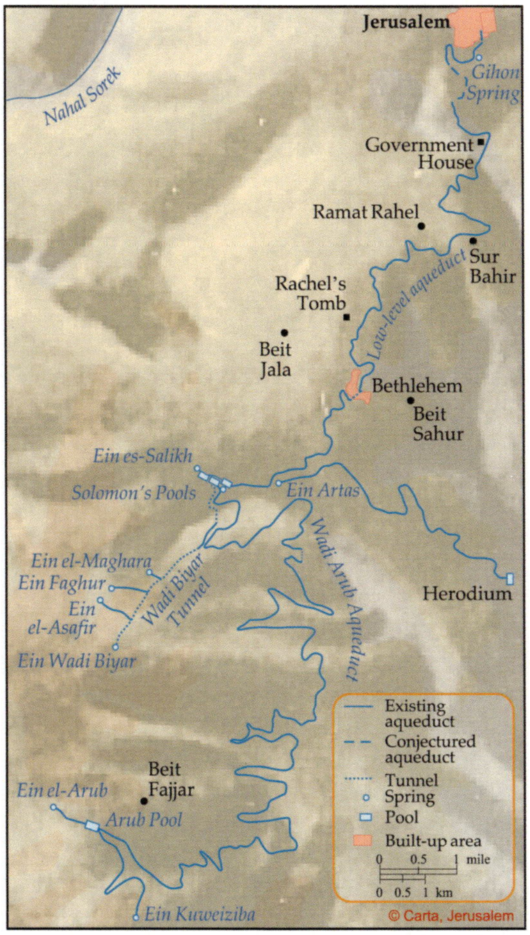

state. But by now the crowds who might have seen Jesus as a deliverer had closed ranks with elements within the religious establishment who wanted him dead, and all called for his execution. Sensing where things were headed, it was better to get rid of Jesus now than to incur the wrath of Rome one more time (Mt 27:20–23). In the end the growing mob pulled the ultimate trump card: "If you release Jesus, you're no friend of Caesar" (Jn 19:12), and *that* was the one thing Pilate couldn't have.

In the end, as the trials and tribulations of a prefect go, Pilate's day could have been worse. His own agenda had been thwarted, it is true, but he had avoided a riot, solved a difficult case to the satisfaction of the accusers (much to his own chagrin, but he would have to live with that), kept Rome out of the matter, saved his own neck in the process (*that* was more important), and been able to throw some barbs at the people who had dared buck his authority in the past. And only one person had to be sacrificed—and he wasn't even a Judean.[54]

By such mixed doses of in-your-face and dodge-and-feint, Pilate rode herd over the Jews under his watch and care. But things couldn't go on indefinitely. Ironically, the sequence of events that led to Pilate's downfall didn't happen in Judea but in Samaria, the portion of his territory that had a sizeable gentile population. An unnamed Samaritan mystic (Josephus, who had no reason to protect Samaritan sensibilities, called him "one who thought lying was a thing of little consequence and who contrived things to please the multitudes"; *Ant.* xviii.85) inspired a crowd to converge on Mount Gerizim and look for sacred vessels that Moses had buried somewhere on the mountain. But they came armed; this was no effort at objective archaeology. Sensing a messianic-type revolt, Pilate sent the army to prevent their ascent up the mountain; some were killed, others fled; many were taken prisoner. Their recondite leader was executed straightaway.

But this time Pilate couldn't outrun the crowds. Even though the official Samaritan leadership likely saw their unfortunate mystic as a bit of a kook, they couldn't let Pilate's attack on their community go unanswered. A delegation reported the matter to Vitellius, governor of the province Syria, claiming that Pilate had murdered members of a harmless crowd. Tired of Pilate's excesses, Vitellius pulled rank and sent him to Rome to finally answer directly to the emperor for his heavy-handed ways (*Ant.* xviii.85–89). While Pilate was en route to Rome, Tiberius died—and with this, the contemporary sources for his life fall silent. We are left to later reflections instead, such as that of Eusebius who in the fourth century A.D. tells us that Pilate committed suicide[55]—if so, it was the honorable solution for a Roman found guilty of crimes against the interest of the state. The spurious but influential *Mors Pilati* ("Death of Pilate"), a Latin document dated no earlier than the fifth century A.D., relates that Pilate's corpse was sunk in Rome's Tiber River but that "malignant and filthy spirits" clinging to his body so agitated the waters that he was drawn out and sunk again in the Rhone near Vienne (in southeastern Gaul). But those waters also churned and so his body was moved to the territory of Lausanne where the evil spirits plagued that land. Pilate's unfortunate remains were finally buried in a pit surrounded by mountains somewhere high in the western Alps "where to this day" reports *Mors Pilati*, "certain diabolical machinations are said to bubble up." In serving Pilate's just desserts, tradition accomplished what history didn't.

PONTIUS PILATE IN HISTORY AND TRADITION

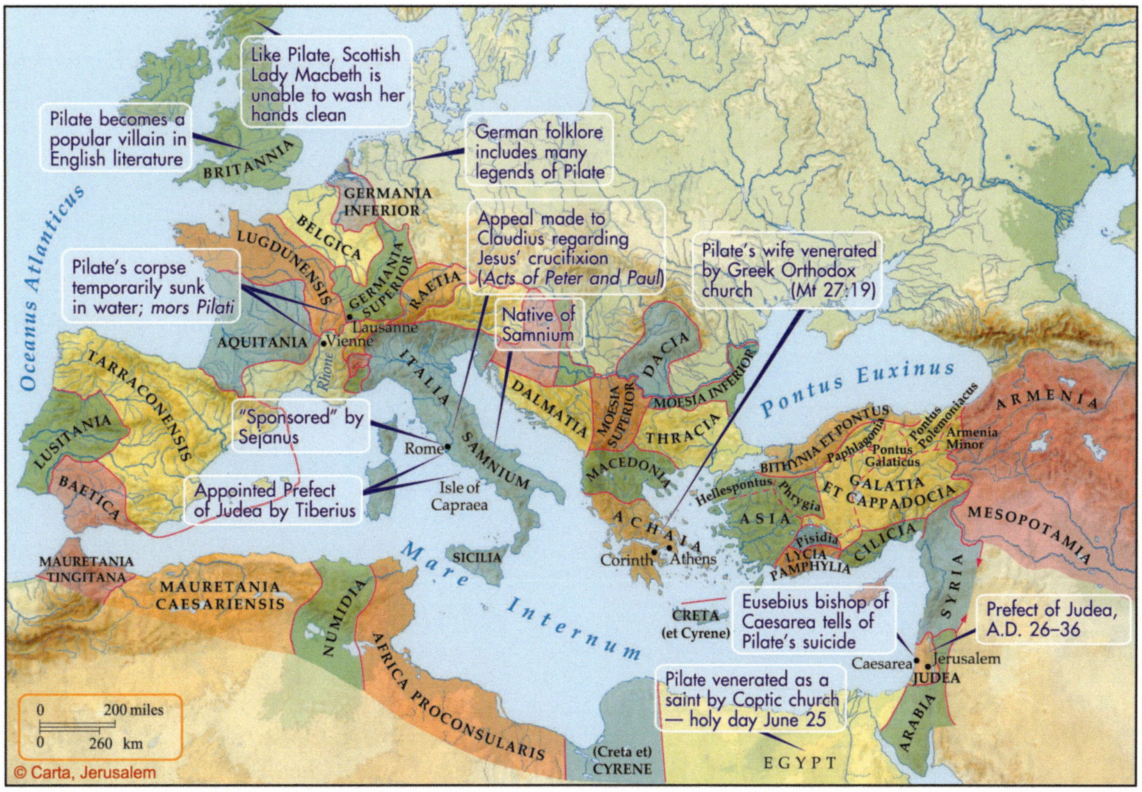

PAUL

Born and reared as Saul from Tarsus, the largest city in Rome's gateway province of Cilicia (Acts 9:11; 22:3), the Apostle Paul was the bridge that carried belief in Jesus as Messiah from a Jerusalem-based Judaism to Gentiles living in "the uttermost parts of the earth" (Acts 1:8; cf. Rom 11:17–24). The world has never been the same for his efforts.

Saul was born probably about a decade after the birth of Jesus, though in a world away. In the first century A.D. Tarsus was a center of Hellenistic education and culture that rivaled Alexandria and Athens in influence.[56] It was, moreover, a major trade center and gateway in the Roman world, as Istanbul is today. As a result, Saul's Tarsus contemporaries were, by definition, "of the world," cosmopolitan and connected. Many of the residents of Tarsus, including some Jews, were granted Roman citizenship by Pompey and Antony in the last half of the first century B.C.; perhaps Saul's father or grandfather was among that number since Paul himself was born a Roman citizen (cf. Acts 21:39).[57] Without question his roots were deeply intertwined with the penetrating reality of the Hellenistic world.

But they were thrust just as deeply into traditional Judaism. Paul's abbreviated autobiography: "[I am] a Hebrew of Hebrews… as to the righteousness which is in *Torah*, blameless" (Phil 3:5–6) suggests that in spite of his family's likely connections to the politics and economy of Tarsus, they also maintained strict control of their Jewishness and were careful not to assimilate too much to the glories of Hellenism that so defined their home town. Both Saul and his father were, after all, Pharisees (Acts 23:6) and remembered their tribal roots in Benjamin (Phil 3:5–6). So Saul moved to Jerusalem early in life where he received a traditional rabbinic education (Acts 22:3; 26:4; cf. Acts 23:16). He was joined to the aged rabbi Gamaliel (the Elder), one of the leading Pharisaic scholars of the day (Acts 22:3). Although his credentials as a teacher of Bible and preserver of rabbinic tradition were impeccable (at one point he had served as president of the Sanhedrin), Gamaliel was also a student of Greek literature and advocated tolerance toward Gentiles. Saul, certainly fluent in Greek, Hebrew (Acts 21:37–40) and Aramaic and arguably conversant in Latin, was one of Gamaliel's prize students. And, like many other Pharisees, Saul also had an income-producing job, in this case a maker of tents (Acts 18:3).[58]

SAUL'S EARLY YEARS

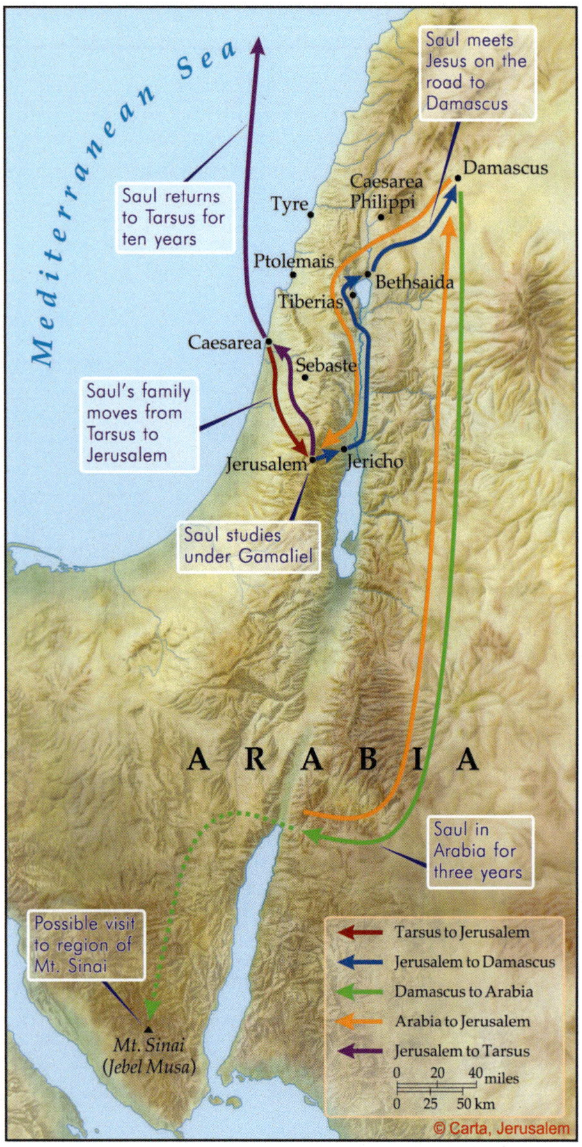

Saul decided to build his reputation as a zealous Pharisee by publicly opposing the new and fast-growing group of Jews (centered in Jerusalem and led by Peter, James and John) who preached that Jesus of Nazareth was the long-awaited Messiah (Acts 3:26; cf. Acts 2:14–36; 3:11–26). Saul gave full ascent to the stoning of Stephen, a leader of the Jesus movement, then imprisoned Stephen's colleagues (Acts 8:3). The community scattered; Saul followed in quick pursuit. Armed with letters of extradition signed by the high priest against any believers in Jesus whom he might find in Damascus, Saul journeyed north (Acts 9:1–2). His route necessarily passed through Jesus-territory (eastern Galilee). Then, as he was approaching Damascus, Saul met the resurrected Jesus as a bright light and a voice of clear command (Acts 9:3–6). On the road to oppose "the Way" (Acts 9:2), Saul fell in stride behind his new Rabbi. The transformation was instant and wholly unexplainable in normal human terms. Saul immediately recognized Jesus as the Son of God, was baptized and began to declare such in the synagogues of the city (Acts 9:7–22; cf. 22:16). His Damascus-road experience was so powerful that Saul repeated it at least twice in his own defense later in life (Acts 22:1–16; 26:9–20).

Saul promptly went into Arabia for three years (Gal 1:17–18), perhaps to sort out the ramifications of his new-found life direction, then made his way back to Damascus (Gal 1:15–17) and, eventually, Jerusalem. There he found himself the subject of all sorts of rumors and innuendos (Acts 9:26). It was sometime in the middle A.D. 30's; Saul was about 30 years old (cf. Lk 3:23). Peter, with Barnabas, took the lead in welcoming him into the community of believers in Jerusalem; it took personalities as strong as Saul himself to convince the fledgling Christian community that he was now one of them (Acts 9:27–28; Gal 1:18–19). Saul's old comrades—the Hellenistic (Greek-speaking) Jews of Jerusalem and likely most of his earlier supporters on the Sanhedrin—were less forgiving and so Saul was hustled off to Caesarea (it would become a familiar port-of-call), then back home to Tarsus by way of the string of ports along the northern Levantine (Syrian) shore (Acts 9:29–30; Gal 1:21).

There followed ten quiet years in the historical record, largely silent but certainly not unproductive. We can easily assume that Saul was active for the sake of the Gospel throughout Cilicia during this time, perfecting his skills in teaching, preaching and persuading both Jews and Gentiles to follow Jesus as the Christ. Throughout, the leaders of the church in Jerusalem heard of Saul's work and were pleased (Gal 1:22–24). The first city to see large numbers of Gentiles come to faith in Jesus as the Messiah was Antioch in Syria, the third largest city in the Roman Empire and one that was well positioned on the trade routes of the eastern Mediterranean.

INTERNATIONAL GATEWAYS OF THE NORTHEASTERN MEDITERRANEAN

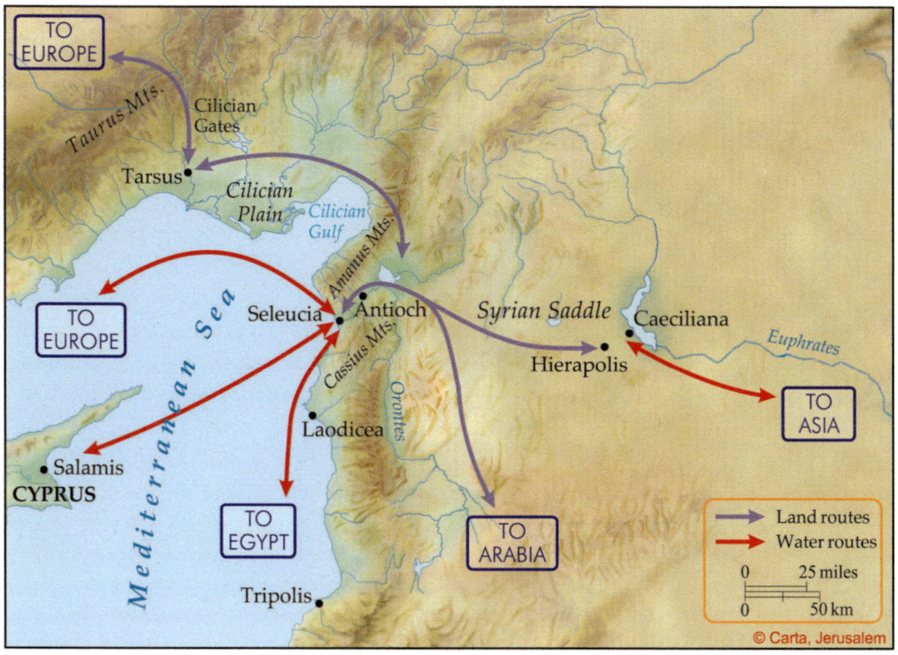

Saul and Barnabas played an instrumental role in the explosive growth of the Antioch church, and it was here that the believers were first called Christians, i.e., followers of *Christos*, the Messiah (Acts 11:9–26).

Saul's first visit to Jerusalem in fourteen years (in A.D. 46?) was for the purpose of bringing relief aid to the community of believers in the city which had been hard struck by famine (Acts 11:27–30; cf. Acts 2:44–45; 4:36–5:1–2; 6:1; 24:17; Rom 15:26–27; 1 Cor 16:1–4).[59] He took advantage of his time in the city to argue forcefully with James, Peter and John for full acceptance of the Gentiles—even those who remained uncircumcised—into the community of the church. In the end it was agreed that Saul would continue to concentrate his efforts on bringing the good news of Jesus to the Gentiles, while the Jerusalem leadership would remain focused on spreading the Gospel to the Jews (Gal 2:1–10; cf. Acts 22:21; Rom 1:14; 16:18). It was a formative, though informal, council. With it, the stage was set for Saul to become the Apostle Paul (Acts 13:9). The curtain rose on a new act in the Gospel story. The scenery had changed: the contained arc of the Fertile Crescent had given way to the vast amphitheatre of the Mediterranean.

Paul (now using his Greek name *Paulos* rather than the Greek form of his Hebrew name, *Saulos*; cf. Acts 13:9) and Barnabas returned to Antioch. They were commissioned by the leaders of Antioch's international church to follow the call of the Holy Spirit (Acts 13:9). The Spirit didn't give details; like Abraham, they were just to go (Acts 13:1–3; cf. Gen 12:1, 4) and, like the patriarch their general direction of travel was to the west, into a land that for them was yet unknown. Paul and his various traveling companions would be constantly on the move, sometimes settling down for a while (Abraham's Beer-sheba would become Paul's Ephesus; his Hebron Paul's Rome) but then journeying on; approaching new places, forging new relationships; no longer at home anywhere but gradually becoming so everywhere in the new land of his divine call—with an unwavering faith in a new covenant and a harvest as vast as the stars of the open Mediterranean sky and the grains of sand along its endless shore: "And if you belong to Christ, then you are Abraham's descendants, heirs according to the promise (Gal 3:29; cf. Gen 15:5; 22:17).

Taking a young John Mark, Barnabas's cousin, as their assistant (Acts 13:5; cf. 12:12; Col 4:10), Paul and Barnabas sailed from Seleucia (Antioch's bustling port) to Cyprus, homeland of Barnabas. Cyprus offered a brilliant mosaic of cultures and people groups hailing from across the eastern Mediterranean, including a large, vibrant and, apparently, relatively tolerant Jewish community. Paul and his small team worked their way from Salamis to Paphos, the provincial capital, teaching in synagogues along the way. This became their *modus operandi*: even though Paul's ministry focused on Gentiles, he typically made contacts first in a city's synagogue (he was still a skilled and personally observant rabbi; cf. Acts 18:18; 20:16; 21:23–26; Rom 1:16; 9:1–5; 10:1–4; 11:1–24). The island's proconsul, Sergius Paulus, was well-acquainted with his Jewish subjects, and as a result of Paul's preaching and miracle-working he responded favorably to the new message about Jesus. Cyprus became the first Roman province to be governed by

PAUL'S FIRST MISSIONARY JOURNEY, C. A.D. 48

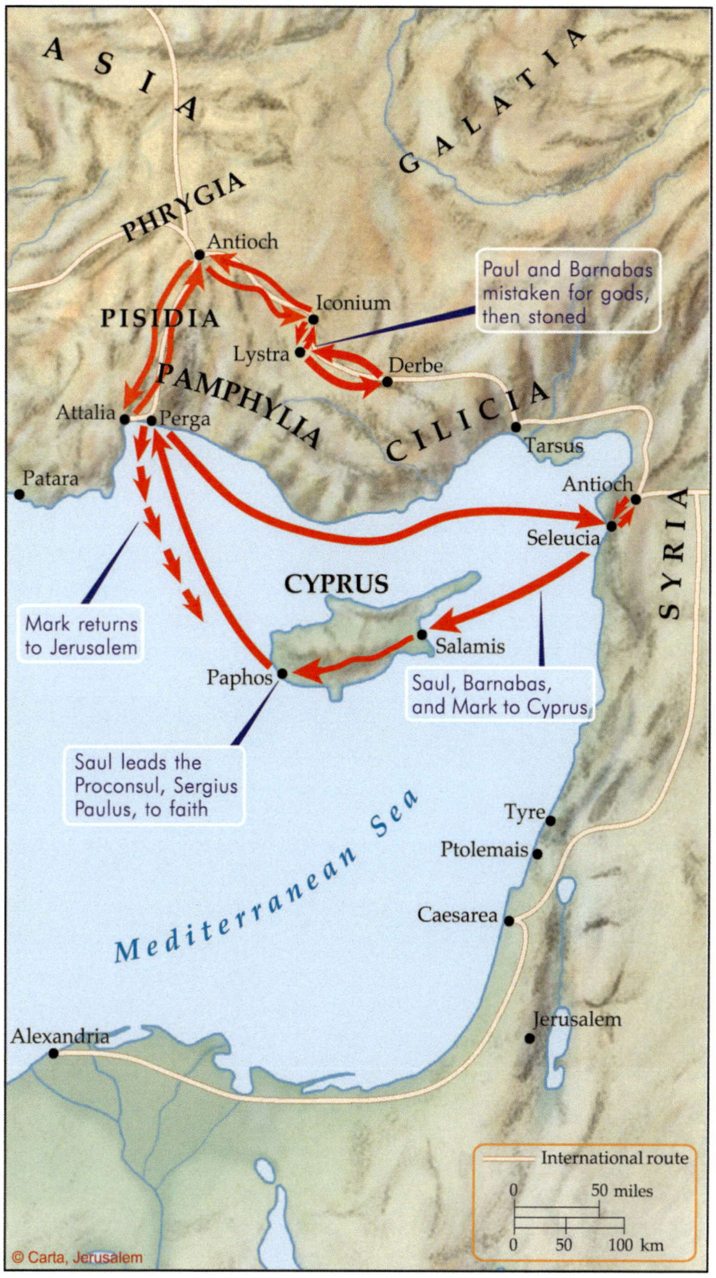

THE JERUSALEM COUNCIL, A.D. 49 OR 50

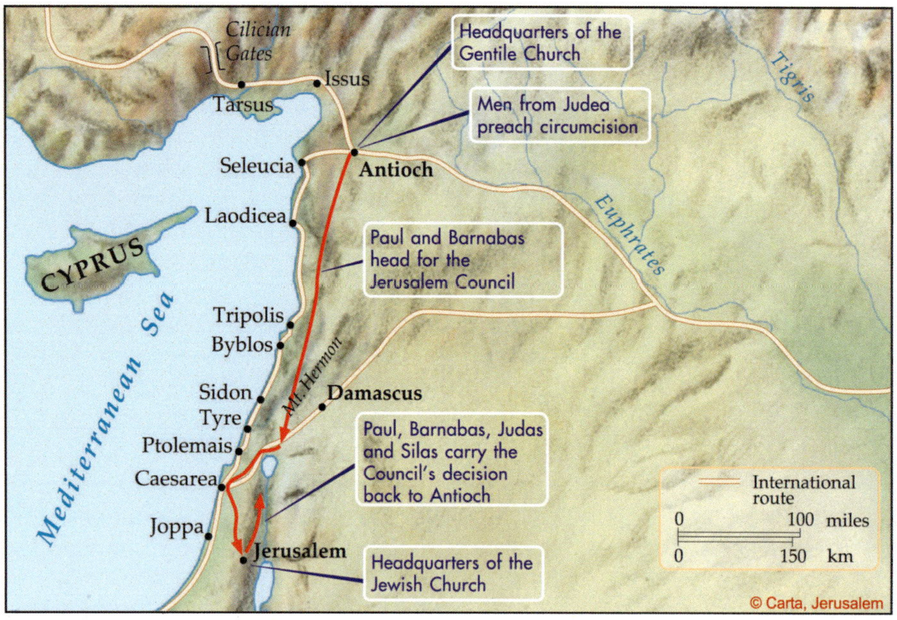

a Christian (Acts 13:4–12); for Paul it couldn't have been a more promising start.

From Paphos Paul and his companions sailed northwest to Perga, a large port city in Pamphylia where for reasons unknown John Mark left them to return to Jerusalem (Acts 13:13). From there they crossed the rugged Taurus Mountains to Psidian Antioch, a moderately-sized city in southern Galatia lying a hard ten-days' walk from the coast (Acts 13:13–14). Arriving in town they naturally headed first to the synagogue where Paul preached a message of Jesus "through whom everyone who believes is freed from all things from which you could not be freed through the *Torah* of Moses" (Acts 13:39). Most of the Jews in attendance were understandably opposed to the message, although Paul's words were generally well received by God-fearing Gentiles (Acts 13:15–49). Facing opposition, Paul and Barnabas fled southeast along the main trade route that connected Galatia with Syria, to Iconium and then Lystra, where his strategy—and the results—were the same (Acts 13:50–14:20). From there he continued on to Derbe where he enjoyed results without opposition (Acts 14:21–23). From there it was a fairly short walk back to Tarsus and Paul likely would have returned home were it not for the positive response he finally had to the Gospel message. Encouraged and emboldened (he actually never lacked for courage), Paul decided instead to retrace his steps the same way he had come (Acts 14:21–28).

The realistic prospect of a gentile-majority in the young church didn't sit well with most of the leadership in Jerusalem and so a delegation arrived in Antioch intent on making the point that gentiles could become part of the church only if, as Jewish proselytes, they were first circumcised (Acts 15:1; Gal 2:11–21). Clearly the Jerusalem church was thinking in terms of belief in Jesus as a movement *within* Judaism rather than something that could—or should—exist on the outside. The term "Christian" had originated in a gentile context and it was time the folks up there acknowledged their connection to Jerusalem. It is likely that these "Judaizers" (as they are often called in the secondary literature) made follow-up visits to the churches that Paul and Barnabas had planted in Galatia, anxious to correct any misinformation that might have been spread in the Apostle's zeal to bring the message of Jesus to both Jew and Greek (cf. Gal 1:6–9; 3:1; 4:12–5:15; 6:12–13). A credible case can be made that Paul wrote his letter to the Galatians—his first epistle, a primer on justification by faith—quickly, from Antioch, in response to these in-house challenges to his work. Paul even went toe-to-toe with Peter on the issue (Gal 2:11–14). The matter was serious enough to prompt a formal discussion in Jerusalem. Paul and Barnabas attended the Jerusalem Council, in A.D. 49 or 50, and argued convincingly for full gentile inclusion, without circumcision, into the otherwise predominantly Jewish church (Acts 15:2–21). The Jerusalem church acquiesced, though not without serious debate, and while the decision paved the way for an inclusive church it also cast the die for an eventual split between church and synagogue.

After a short stay in Antioch, likely still in A.D. 50, Paul asked Barnabas to accompany him on a return trip to the churches they had established in Galatia. Barnabas wanted to bring his cousin John Mark along; Paul point-blank refused, remembering too clearly John Mark's bailout back in Perga (Acts 15:36–38; cf. 13:13). After a sharp disagreement, Barnabas and John Mark returned to Cyprus to focus on spreading the Gospel in their homeland, while Paul tapped Silas, a leader of the Jerusalem church and a Roman citizen, instead (Acts 15:22, 32; 16:37). The two set off overland to Galatia (Acts 15:39–41), picking up a young Timothy in Lystra on the way (Acts

The Mysian port of Troas; the site today is called Eskistanbul (Old Stambul), a small town and pier nestled in expansive though largely overgrown ruins of the ancient site.

The Areopagus is a large hill of rough limestone, mostly bare today, rising just west of—and overshadowed by—Athen's famed Acropolis.

PAUL'S SECOND MISSIONARY JOURNEY, A.D. 50–52

16:1–3). The result: two teams in the field rather than one, a net gain for the early church.

Paul and Timothy were joined by Luke, "the beloved physician," at Troas, a lively port on the Aegean just south of the Hellespont (Acts 16:4–8; Col 4:14). Luke would travel with Paul intermittently, chronicling not only their journeys together but the earliest history of the church (the book of Acts). At Troas, just south of the spot that Alexander the Great (of Macedon) had entered Asia to spread the glories of Hellenism across the East, Paul had a vision compelling him to travel over to Macedonia and preach the Gospel on European soil (Acts 16:9–10). Gladly heeding his "Macedonian call," Paul and his companions sailed to Neapolis, Macedonia's easternmost port. Thirteen miles inland, over a low rise, lay the grand plain of Philippi, dominated by the city of the same name, the first European objective of the Apostle and his three protégés. Philippi had been founded as a Greek city by Alexander's father in 360 B.C.[60] The world view of Moses that the golden-haired conqueror had tried to overwhelm with the seductive beauties of Hellenism was about to invade his father's namesake city. Here Paul met and baptized Lydia of Thyatira, who became the first Christian convert in Europe (Acts 16:13–15). Local opposition landed Paul and Silas in prison; they were freed by an opportune earthquake, then formally released the next morning by the city's magistrates (Acts 16:22–34). The church in Philippi would become one of Paul's favorites, and supported him generously along his way (cf. Phil 1:3–11; 4:15–16).

From there the trio traveled the *Via Egnatia* to Thessalonica, capital of Macedonia, and quickly established another church. Again opposition drove Paul on, this time due to the charge that he was teaching things contrary to the decrees of Caesar (Acts 17:1-9). Paul eventually made his way to Athens, where he stayed just long enough to take in the city's famed sights; he considered them hollow compared to the glories of the kingdom of Jesus. In spite of preaching a spirited sermon on Mars Hill, Paul failed to make significant inroads among Athens' erudite population (Acts 17:16-34) and so headed over to the bawdy port city of Corinth instead. Here he found a bustling boomtown badly in need of redemption, and was fascinated. He stayed for eighteen months (Acts 18:1, 11).

Paul had more visible success in Corinth than perhaps anywhere (with the possible exception of Ephesus, which he would visit later). One of his converts was Crispus, a leader of the synagogue, but most believers came from the lower classes of society, folks who were not very wise, mighty or noble, or who had been out-and-out scoundrels (1 Cor 1:26; 6:9–11). The church in Corinth grew mightily, but had special needs (bad habits were hard to break) and Paul eventually wrote as many as four letters to them urging unity and clean living (Acts 18:1–17; cf. 1 Cor 5:9; 2 Cor 7:8). Eventually heading home, Paul's ship put into the port of Ephesus where he stayed just long enough to be missed. He then sailed largely open-sea to Caesarea and reported to the church leaders up in Jerusalem, returning to Antioch sometime in late A.D. 52, his second missionary journey completed (Acts 18:18–22).

The church in Antioch was no doubt pleased with what they heard, and Paul could scarcely wait to head out again. His focus would continue to be on the Empire's imperial routes and its major cities where strategically-placed churches would grow and carry the Gospel into the surrounding countryside. Sometime in A.D. 53 he set off overland through Galatia and Phrygia again, likely retracing

The Roman theater at Ephesus.

PAUL'S THIRD MISSIONARY JOURNEY, A.D. 53–57

earlier steps and renewing old and dear acquaintances in Derbe, Lystra, Iconium and Psidian Antioch (Acts 18:23) before settling in Ephesus (Acts 19:1). Paul remained in Ephesus for up to three years (Acts 19:8, 10; 20:31; cf. Acts 18:20–21). There he found "a wide door for effective service" (1 Cor 16:8–9) and used the city as a base of operations to reach people from all areas of Asia Minor (Acts 19:10, 26). Years later, when he was a prisoner in Rome, Paul wrote his letter to the Ephesians, a mature treatise on the blessings and responsibilities of living the Christian life. One gets the feeling that he gained great satisfaction from his work in there. Eventually pressure from citizens loyal to Artemis, the city's patron deity, drove Paul out of town, partly for his own safety, partly for the sake of the church (Acts 19:23–20:1).

Sometime in A.D. 55 or 56 Paul made his way back into Macedonia (Acts 20:1; 2 Cor 2:12–13). At this point the data is scattered and it is not possible to trace his subsequent travels with any degree of certainty, although he did spend time on more than one occasion tending to matters in freewheeling Corinth, where old temptations were ever fresh. He also made it as far west as Illyricum (today's east Adriatic coast; cf. Rom 15:19).

Paul longed to visit Rome and even more distant places such as Spain, but first wanted to make a trip back to Jerusalem for Pentecost (Shavuot; Rom 15:22–25; cf. Acts 19:21). He retraced his steps through Achaia and Macedonia to Asia Minor but, sensing that if he stopped at Ephesus he would likely never get away, he sailed on to Miletus. There he met the leaders of the church of Ephesus for a heart-wrenching farewell: "I know that all of you will no longer see my face…and [so] commend you to God" (Acts 20:18–35).

Clearing customs at Caesarea, Paul made it up to Jerusalem for Pentecost (Acts 20:36–21:8. There he gave a glowing report of the spread of the Gospel among the gentiles (Acts 21:18–19). A quarter century had passed since the Pentecost when the Holy Spirit had first empowered the earliest believers in Jesus, and over the years the church had grown with remarkable success.

But the issue of to what extent gentiles who had come to faith in Jesus should keep normative Jewish religious practices remained very much alive. Paul himself willingly visited the *miqveh* in Jerusalem for ritual purification, then sponsored temple sacrifices for four Jewish believers who were finishing a period of vows (Acts 21:20–26). In the process, he was accused of bringing a gentile into the temple. To avoid a mass disturbance, Paul was plucked out by a squadron of Roman soldiers, then gave an impassioned, public defense of his ministry. Following a formal hearing before the Sanhedrin (Acts 21:27–23:11), the case was transferred to the Roman procurator Felix (A.D. 52–60?) down in Caesarea due to a threat on Paul's life. There he was sequestered in Herod's Praetorium (Acts 23:12–35).

Felix kept Paul under arrest for two years, partly hoping for the customary bribe that might spring him free, partly to let impassioned feelings back in Jerusalem subside. Paul took advantage of the situation and met Felix often for talks at the highest levels (Acts 24:1–26). The case was revived in A.D. 60 when the new procurator, Porcius Festus, made the customary rounds to inquire as to the status of privileges and rights in his realm. The result was a full-blown hearing during which Paul gave an impassioned defense of his actions before Festus, the leadership of Jerusalem's Jewish communities and Agrippa II, the last monarch of the old Herodian dynasty. It ended with him appealing directly to Caesar (according

Paul likely passed through the region of Colossae on his third missionary journey, perhaps founding and certainly encouraging the church in the city.

Ruins of the picturesque city of Assos, where Paul rejoined ship for his springtime journey to Caesarea.

to the right of a Roman citizen), thereby gaining free passage to the city to which he longed to go all along (Acts 25:1–26:32). If Caesar Nero would agree to judge his case, Paul could gain official recognition of Christianity as a viable sect (in Paul's eyes, as "the fulfillment") of Judaism.

It was already late in the shipping season and the Mediterranean's unpredictable weather patterns nearly sank his last voyage. A series of massive storms battered the ship, a large Alexandrian freighter at open sea for fourteen days, before it ran aground off the small island of Malta, beneath Sicily (Acts 27:1–44). Ship and cargo were both lost; the passengers all made it safely to shore where they spent the winter under the hospitality of the islanders (Acts 28:1–10). Resuming the journey the next spring, Paul finally entered the heart of the Roman Empire early in A.D. 61. Placed under loose house arrest and living at his own expense, he openly preached the Gospel of Jesus for two years to all who would hear (Acts 28:11–31).

The book of Acts—the best and only connected source on the life of the Apostle Paul—ends here. In one sense it is enough—the Gospel had reached the center of "the uttermost part of the earth" (cf. Acts 1:8) and its greatest advocate and ambassador was speaking its tenants freely. Yet questions remain, the most pressing of which is what happened to Paul in Rome. All evidence agrees that he was eventually executed by Nero—his Roman citizenship granted him rights of status, protection and appeal in life, but also dictated that if execution should come, it be by beheading with the sword.[61] But *when* Paul was martyred, and what he may have accomplished in the meantime, remains a matter of speculation. He (and Peter) certainly succumbed either during Nero's first great persecution of the church in A.D. 64, or sometime within the next two or at most three years. Scraps of evidence suggest that Paul may have been released from Rome after his initial imprisonment and traveled again in the Mediterranean (to Crete—Tit 1:5; Macedonia again—1 Tim 1:3; and Nicopolis in Epirus, on the Adriatic side of Achaea—Tit 3:12) or even to Spain (cf. Rom 15:22–25 and 1 Clement 5:7). Sufficient time is also needed for Paul to have composed most or all of his epistles to the churches in Ephesus, Philippi, Colossae and Laodicea, and letters to Philemon, Timothy (twice) and Titus. Like with all great men, some dreams must have been left on the table.

What is clear by all accounts is that Paul was a man of faith, and faithfulness (Rom 5:20; cf. Rom 7:7–20). His life was overly full with opportunity, but also challenge. Dangers of every kind lay ever at hand—if it wasn't the road, it was the people on it, or at its end (2 Cor 11:23–29). Being all things to all people yet unwaveringly true to the call of Jesus was humanly nearly impossible. Yet Paul succeeded, and the extent to which he did is measured in large part by the measure of grace with which his life was filled.

PAUL'S JOURNEY TO ROME, A.D. 60 (FALL) TO 61 (SPRING)

NOTES AND REFERENCES

1 Examples of the theory and practice of telling and retelling biblical narratives are many. The following works are a representative selection: Meir Sternberg, *The Poetics of Biblical Narrative* (Bloomington: Indiana University Press, 1985); Herbert Chanan Brichto, *Toward a Grammar of Biblical Poetics* (New York: Oxford University Press, 1992); John A. Beck, *God as Storyteller* (St. Louis: Chalice Press, 2008); Maurice Samuel, *Certain People of the Book* (New York: Union of American Hebrew Congregations, 1955); and Elie Wiesel, *Five Biblical Portraits* (South Bend: University of Notre Dame Press, 1981).

2 The descriptive phrase "land between" for the southern Levant is that of Jim Monson, *Regions on the Run* (Rockford, IL: Biblical Backgrounds, 1998), 6.

3 See for instance M. B. Rowton, "Autonomy and Nomadism in Western Asia," *Orientalis* NS 42 (1973): 247–258 and "Dimorphic Structure and Topology," *Oriens Antiquus* 15 (1976): 17–31.

4 While specifics will always be debated, the broad stroke context of the patriarchal narratives still fits nicely within the known context of first half of second millennium B.C. Mesopotamia and Egypt. See K. A. Kitchen, *On the Reliability of the Old Testament* (Grand Rapids: Eerdmans, 2003), 316–372.

5 John H. Sailhamer, *The Pentateuch as Narrative* (Grand Rapids: Zondervan, 1992), 110–111.

6 For instance see John Bright, *A History of Israel*, 3d ed. (Philadelphia: Westminster, 1981), 87.

7 Nicholas Grimal, *A History of Egypt,* transl. by Ian Shaw (Oxford: Blackwell, 1994), 245–292.

8 Morris Bierbrier, *The Tomb-Builders of the Pharaohs* (Cairo: American University Press, 1982).

9 John D. Currid, *Ancient Egypt and the Old Testament* (Grand Rapids: Baker, 1997), 104–120.

10 Menashe Har-El, *The Sinai Journeys: The Route of the Exodus* (San Diego: Ridgefield, 1983).

11 Yigal Yadin, *Hazor: The Head of All Those Kingdoms* (London: Oxford, 1972); Wayne Horowitz and Takayoshi Oshima, *Cuneiform in Canaan* (Jerusalem: Israel Exploration Society, 2006), 65–87.

12 Amnon Ben-Tor, "Hazor," in *The New Encyclopedia of Archaeological Excavations in the Holy Land* (*NEAEHL*) (Jerusalem: Israel Exploration Society, 1993, 2008), 1769–1773.

13 Abraham Faust, *Israel's Ethnogenesis: Settlement, Interaction, Expansion and Resistance* (London: Equinox, 2006).

14 Eilat Mazar, *The Palace of King David* (Jerusalem: Shoham Academic Research, 2009); and Ronny Reich, *Excavating the City of David* (Jerusalem: Israel Exploration Society, 2011), 265–268.

15 John Monson, "The New 'Ain Dara Temple: Closest Solomonic Parallel," *Biblical Archaeology Review* 26/3 (2000): 20–35, 67.

16 Anson F. Rainey and R. Steven Notley, *The Sacred Bridge: Carta's Atlas of the Biblical World* (Jerusalem: Carta, 2006), 174–178.

17 Note for instance the Black Obelisk of Shalmaneser; Mordechai Cogan, *The Raging Torrent: Historical Inscriptions from Assyria and Babylonia Relating to Ancient Israel* (Jerusalem: Carta, 2008), 22–27; cf. 27–30.

18 Credit to Omri is given in the Mesha Stele (Moabite Stone), which provides an alternative, though supporting, view of the biblical record of events. See Shmuel Aḥituv, *Echoes from the Past: Hebrew and Cognate Inscriptions from the Biblical Period* (Jerusalem: Carta, 2008), 389–418.

19 Albert T. Olmstead, "The Calculated Frightfulness of Ashur-nasir-pal," *Journal of the American Oriental Society* 38 (1918): 209–263.

20 Cogan, *The Raging Torrent*, 13–22.

21 Aḥituv, *Echoes from the Past*, 389–418.

22 Childs, Brevard S. *Isaiah: A Commentary* (Louisville: Westminster / John Knox, 2001).

23 Babylonian Talmud, *Megillah* 10b.

24 Rainey and Notley, *The Sacred Bridge*, 226–227.

25 Cogan, *The Raging Torrent*, 74–79.

26 Abraham J. Heschel, *The Prophets,* vol. 1 (New York: Harper Torchbooks, 1962), 5.

27 Nahman Avigad, *Discovering Jerusalem* (Jerusalem: Israel Exploration Society, 1980), 31–54.

28 Cogan, *The Raging Torrent*, 103–105; Rainey and Notley, *The Sacred Bridge*, 235.

29 David Ussishkin, "Lachish," *NEAEHL*, 905–909.

30 Cogan, *The Raging Torrent*, 111–127.

31 An Assyrian title, either "chief butler" or, perhaps better, "field commander."

32 Cogan, *The Raging Torrent*, 115.

33 For instance H. W. F. Saggs, *The Might that Was Assyria* (London: Sidgwick & Jackson, 1984), 107.

34 Rudolf Cohen, "Kadesh-barnea," *NEAEHL*, 846–847.

35 Miriam Aharoni, "Arad—The Israelite Citadels," *NEAEHL*, 82–83.

36 Frank M. Cross, "el-Buqei'a," *NEAEHL*, 267–269.

37 Joseph Naveh, "Ḥashavyahu, Meẓad," *NEAEHL*, 585–586.

38 Yigal Shiloh, "Megiddo," *NEAEHL*, 1023.

39 Alfred Edersheim, *The Life and Times of Jesus the Messiah* (Grand Rapids: Eerdmans, 1956), 133–138.

40 An alternative view places the ministry of John the Baptist further north, in Galilee and the province of Batanea beyond the Jordan; see Rainey and Notley, *The Sacred Bridge*, 350–351.

41 Joseph A. Fitzmyer, "Qumran Messianism," ch. 5 in *The Dead Sea Scrolls and Christian Origins* (Grand Rapids: Eerdmans, 2000), 73–110.

42 Ken M. Campbell, "What Was Jesus' Occupation?" *Journal of the Evangelical theological Society* 48 (2005): 501–519.

43 R. M. Nagy, et al., eds., *Sepphoris in Galilee: Crosscurrents of Culture* (Raleigh: North Carolina Museum of Art, 1996).

44 For instance David Flusser, *Jesus* (Jerusalem: Magnes Press, 1997), 28.

45 Josephus, *Life* 349, Pliny, *Nat. Hist.* 5.16; Eusebius, *Onomasticon*, 80.16).

46 Cf. Mishnah, *Bekhoroth* 7.1–7.

47 *Mekhilta de-Rabbi Ishmael, Shabbata* 1.27–28, commenting on Exodus 31:14; and *Shabbata* 1.30.

48 Mishnah, *Sanhedrin*, 7.4; cf. 7.5.

49 Several contemporary writers described the horrors of crucifixion, including Pseudo-Manetho, *Apotelesmatica* 4:198–199; Juvenal, *Satires*, 14.77–78; Martial, *Liber Spectaculorum*, 7; and Quintilian, *Declamationes*, 274.

50 Menahem Stern, *Greek and Latin Authors on Jews and Judaism*, vol. 2 (Jerusalem: Israel Academy of Sciences and Humanities, 1980), 92.

51 S. Safrai and M. Stern, eds., *The Jewish People in the First Century* (Assen: Van Gorcum, 1973), 318, 349–350.

52 Philo, *De legatione ad Gaium*, 301–303.

53 Philo, *De legatione ad Gaium*, 299–305.

54 For a similar analysis emphasizing the riptide of competing egos and conflicting political agendas see Ellis Rivkin, *What Crucified Jesus? The Political Execution of a Charismatic* (Nashville: Abingdon, 1984).

55 Eusebius, *Historica ecclesiastica* ii.7.

56 Strabo, *Geography*, xiv.5.13.

57 In a tradition that cannot be verified, Jerome relates that Paul's ancestors had migrated to Tarsus from Gischala in Upper Galilee when Pompey conquered Judea in 63 B.C.; *De viris illustribus* 5.

58 Mishnah, *Kiddushin* 4.14; *Pirke Avot* 2.2.

59 The decade of the 40's A.D. was in general a time of poor harvests and economic scarcity across the Roman world (Dio Cassius, *Roman History*, lx.11; Suetonius, *Claudius* 18; Tacitus, *Annals* xi.4; xiii.43).

60 Diodoros Siculus, *History*, xvi.8.

61 1 Clement 5:5–7; Eusebius, *Historia ecclesiastica* ii.25.6. The late (sixth century A.D.) *Acts of Peter and Paul* (80) provides the requisite details of the execution as the Church remembered them at the time.